D0064686

Rocking Around
the Clock

E. ANN KAPLAN

Rocking Around the Clock

MUSIC TELEVISION, POSTMODERNISM, AND CONSUMER CULTURE

Routledge
New York and London

First published in 1987 by
Methuen, Inc.
Published in Great Britain by
Methuen & Co. Ltd
Reprinted 1988 by Routledge,
11 New Fetter Lane, London EC4P 4EE
29 West 35th Street, New York NY 10001

Typeset in Great Britain
by Boldface Typesetters, 17a Clerkenwell Road, London EC1
Printed in Great Britain
by Richard Clay Ltd, Bungay, Suffolk

Library of Congress Cataloging in Publication Data

Kaplan, E. Ann.
  Rocking around the clock.
  Bibliography: p.
  Includes index
  1. Rock videos — United States. 2. MTV Networks.
  1. Title.
  PN1992.8.M87K36   1987   791.45′75′0973   86-33113

ISBN 0 416 33370 2
     0 415 03005 6 (pbk.)

British Library Cataloguing in Publication Data

Kaplan, E. Ann.
  Rocking around the clock: music television,
  postmodernism and consumer culture.
  1. MTV
  1. Title
  384.55′56′0973   HE8700.72.U6

ISBN 0 416 33370 2
     0 415 03005 6

Contents

Acknowledgments

My very first thanks go to my daughter, Brett Kaplan, who first introduced me to MTV, although she has since moved on to other music. Interviews with Brett, Leo Margolf, and their friends, as well as with Paul Charney and his friends, helped me to understand how MTV was being received by some teenagers in 1984–5.

I next want to thank my good friend, Allon White, for the wonderful discussions during his visit to Rutgers University in 1983; many of my ideas for this book were generated in the course of our talks.

Martin Hoffman has been a constant source of encouragement and support in the writing of this book; he has borne many an hour of videos when he might have preferred other things, and helped me think ideas through when I came to an impasse.

I want to thank for their useful comments the Rutgers students who participated in seminars where MTV was briefly touched on. Gene Sobzchak was particularly helpful. Thanks also to the many students and faculty who came to all the talks on Music Television that I have given over the past few years; their thought-provoking comments, criticisms, and questions made me rethink some positions.

Peggy Phelan has been a thoughtful reader of various papers written as I was developing my ideas, and, in bringing MTV as a critical object to the attention of her graduate students at New York University, she has helped to develop interest in the area. She has also been invaluable in helping me locate specific videos and letting me borrow her tapes.

I want to thank music video director Eddie Barbarini for an illuminating interview, and both he and cameraman Bob Lechterman for allowing me to watch a video being made. Dr York, the producer of that video, also deserves thanks for being interviewed on the set.

I would like to thank the following book and journal editors for permission to reprint, in revised form, articles of mine that they published: first, Philip Drummond and Richard Paterson, editors of *Television in Transition* (London: British Film Institute, 1985) for "A postmodern play of the signifier? Advertising, pastiche and schizophrenia in music television"; the editors of *Journal of Communication Inquiry*, vol. 10, no. 1 (Winter 1986), for "History, the historical spectator and gender address in music television"; the editors of *The Oxford Literary Review*, vol. 8, nos 1–2 (Summer 1986), for "Sexual difference, visual pleasure and the construction of the spectator in music television"; and finally Deidre Pribram, editor of *Cinematic Pleasure and the Female Spectator* (London: Verso, 1987) for "Whose imaginary? Text, body and narrative in select rock videos."

I would have liked to be in a position to thank MTV Publicity for talking to me about their side of things, but unfortunately my calls were never returned. I therefore had to rely on secondary sources in making my comments.

My thanks to the various publicity departments of record companies (under whose labels videos were produced) for their patient supplying of information I needed; I also want to thank the Music Department at *Rolling Stone* magazine for helping out with missing details for my Videography.

I want to thank the following rock stars and record companies for permission to print stills from the following videos: Madonna and Warner Bros Records for stills from "Material Girl" and "Papa Don't Preach"; Bruce Springsteen for stills from "Born In The USA," "Glory Days," and "I'm On Fire"; Motley Crue and Elektra Records for stills from "Smokin' In The Boys' Room" and "Home Sweet Home"; Tina Turner and Capitol Records for stills from "What's Love Got To Do With It" and "Private Dancer"; John Cougar Mellencamp and Riva/Polygram Records for stills from

ACKNOWLEDGMENTS

"Authority Song" and "Hurts So Good"; Pat Benatar and Chrysalis Records for stills from "Love Is A Battlefield"; Elektra Records and The Cars for stills from "You Might Think"; Peter Gabriel and Geffen Records for the still from "Sledgehammer"; Tom Petty and the Heartbreakers and MCA Records for the still from "Don't Come Around Here No More"; Artists Against Apartheid and Manhattan Records for the still from "Sun-City."

I want to thank John Kline (New York Department of Photography) for his work photographing stills for "You Might Think," "Smokin' in the Boys' Room," "Home Sweet Home," "Sledgehammer," "Born in the USA," "Glory Days," "I'm On Fire," "Hurts So Good," "Authority Song," "What's Love Got To Do With It?," "Don't Come Around Here No More." Other stills photographed by Patti Sapone (Blakely/Sapone Productions).

Finally, my thanks to those people in video departments of record companies who tried patiently to track down dates when videos were released. Mark Rodriguez at Capitol Records was particularly helpful, as was Catherine Berclau at Atlantic Records.

Introduction

STRUCTURE AND CONTENT OF MTV

This book is concerned with rock videos as exhibited through Music Television – MTV – as an institution. What I have to say about rock videos only applies directly to their presentation within the MTV context. The textual analyses naturally stand on their own to a degree, and points made in those parts of the book have implications beyond MTV as an institution. But the larger arguments about postmodernism and spectatorship only make sense within the discussion of MTV as a commercial, popular institution, and as a specifically *televisual* apparatus. I will briefly address both issues, whose full implications will emerge as the book progresses

MTV is a 24-hour, non-stop, commercial cable channel, beamed via satellite across the United States and devoted to presenting rock music videos around the clock. Originally owned by Warner Amex Satellite Entertainment Company (WASEC – the station has recently been purchased by Viacom International), MTV is an advertiser-supported, basic cable service for which subscribers do not pay extra. As of Spring 1986, the channel reached 28 million households[1] (it is available wherever there are cable systems to hook it up). The brain child of Robert Pittman, WASEC's then Executive Vice President,[2] MTV was begun in 1981 for an initial cost of $20 million. MTV earned $7 million in ad revenue in the first eighteen months, and in May 1983 the station already had 125 advertisers representing 200 products including Pepsico and Kellogg, that bought air time

1

for spots from 30 to 120 seconds at a cost of from $1500 to $6000.[3] By 1984 the audience had grown to 22 million, aged between 12 and 34, and ad revenue had reached one million a week.[4] By the end of 1983 the channel had $20 million in ad revenue, and figures for 1984 show more than one million a week in ad revenue, with an audience of 18 to 22 million.[5]

In August 1984, MTV became a public corporation and announced that it had agreements with four record companies for exclusive rights to new videos. It was in response to Turner Broadcasting Company's announcement that it would initiate a competing 24-hour music television station that MTV opened its second channel, VH-1 (intended for what Robert Pittman called "an untapped new audience," namely that between the ages of 25 and 49), for an initial cost of $5 million.[6]

Pittman's genius was in imagining, and then implementing, the concept of a 24-hour station devoted entirely to rock videos. For, while rock videos existed before MTV, they were largely tapes of live performances, played on late-night television and mainly used for publicity purposes (the Beatles' "Strawberry Fields" video made in 1967 is an exception in anticipating the contemporary surrealist/ fictional tape). Some Top Twenty programs also featured videos, but it is only since the invention of MTV that regular channels like NBC and ABC have featured rock video programs (e.g. NBC's "Friday Night Videos" and ABC's "Hot Tracks") and other cable channels, like Channel 3 in New York, have put on programs like "Video Box" and "Video Soul," which, like "Hot Tracks," feature mainly black artists. Since MTV, Feature Film Cable channels like HBO also run rock videos between films (HBO has a spot called "Video Jukebox") and USA Cable Network runs videos on its "Night Flight." The recent home VCR boom has now brought increased access to rock videos through the cassette market. A new cable channel – U-68 – is recently available in the East Coast area, featuring videos considered too "avant-garde" for MTV (this channel recently abandoned its rock video format). The Apollo Entertainment Network has produced a series of taped concerts from the renovated Harlem Apollo Theatre, filling in the gap in airplay time for black bands.

These other television sites for video music, then, attempt to

2

remedy the gaps left by MTV's particular "format" – as Bob Pittman calls it when questions are raised. MTV essentially duplicates FM Radio's white rock focus, although FM has perhaps more variety than the cable channel. Clearly Pittman is pleased with the mix of heavy metal, new wave, and pop that he has managed to produce, but people predict that there will be a series of specialized channels in the future, including a jazz-blues channel and a black pop/funk channel, to fill in the gaps. MTV Networks have already begun the trend in their second channel, VH-1, that features "pop" as against "rock" music – a broader category that permits black artists to get airplay. (These issues will all be discussed in more detail later on.)

If MTV is enmeshed in discourses about rock music, it is the insertion of these discourses in the specifically *televisual* apparatus that produces a result drastically different from prior organizations of rock. By "televisual apparatus" I mean: the technological features of the machine itself (the way it produces and presents images); the various "texts," including ads, commentaries, and displays; the central relationship of programming to the sponsors, whose own texts – the ads – are arguably the *real* TV texts;[7] and, finally, the reception sites – which may be anywhere from the living room to the bathroom.

Research on individual aspects of this apparatus has already begun. For instance, scholars may focus on problems of enunciation, that is, who speaks a particular TV text and to whom it is addressed; or look at the manner in which we watch TV (who *controls* the set when it is watched) and at the meanings of its presence in the home; or they may study the so-called "flow" of the programs, the fragmentation of the viewing experience even within any one given program, and the unusual phenomenon of endlessly serialized programs; or, finally, scholars may investigate the ideology embedded in the forms of production and reception, which are not "neutral" or "accidental" but a crucial result of television's overarching commercial framework.

One of the as yet unresolved issues in such research is that of the degree to which theories recently devised for the classical Hollywood cinema are pertinent to the very different televisual apparatus. One striking way that the televisual differs from the filmic apparatus is in the prevalence of programs that are "serials" in one form or another – that is, continuous segments to be viewed daily or weekly. The most obvious are soaps or prime-time dramas, but, stretching the idea a bit, we should also include the news (regularly slotted and so highly stylized as to be "drama"[8]) and the game shows, which are equally stylized. All of these programs exist on a kind of horizontal axis that is never ending, instead of being discrete units consumed within the fixed two-hour limit of the Hollywood movie or, like the novel, having a fixed and clearly defined boundary.

In a sense, TV has neither a clear boundary nor a fixed textual limit. Rather, the TV screen may be conceived of as a frame through which a never ending series of texts moves laterally; it is as though one turned a film strip on its side and pulled the "frames" (episodes on TV) through a strip projector that way instead of vertically. Peggy Phelan presents an alternative metaphor of Foucault's Panopticon, in which the guard surveys a series of prisoners through their windows. She sees the TV producer as the "guard" and the individual TV viewer as the "prisoner who watches in a sequestered and observed solitude."[9]

The "guard" metaphor also works well for the spectator's relationship to the various episodes (serialized programs of various kinds) that represent, in Foucault's words, "a multiplicity that can be numbered and supervised." For the spectator has the *illusion* of being in control of the "windows," whereas in fact the desire for plenitude that keeps him/her watching is, in this case, forever deferred. The TV is seductive precisely because it speaks to a desire that is insatiable – it promises complete knowledge in some far distant and never-to-be-experienced future. TV's strategy is to keep us endlessly consuming in the hopes of fulfilling our desire.

MTV's programming strategies embody the extremes of what is inherent in the televisual apparatus. The channel hypnotizes more than others because it consists of a series of extremely short (four minutes or less) texts that maintain us in an excited state of expectation. The "coming up next" mechanism that is the staple of all serials is an intrinsic aspect of the minute-by-minute MTV watching. We are trapped by the constant hope that the next video will finally satisfy and, lured by the seductive promise of immediate plenitude, we keep endlessly consuming the short texts. MTV thus carries to an extreme a phenomenon that characterizes most of television. The "decentering" experience of viewing produced by the constant alternation of texts is exacerbated on MTV because its *longest* text is the four-minute video.

Later on in the book, I will be extending this discussion so as to clarify precisely the nature of the televisual "imaginary" as against the filmic one. I will be arguing that MTV reproduces a kind of decenteredness, often called "postmodernist," that increasingly reflects young people's condition in the advanced stage of highly developed, technological capitalism evident in America. As an apparatus developed only in recent decades, TV may be seen as at once preparing for and embodying a postmodern consciousness. MTV arguably addresses the desires, fantasies, and anxieties of young people growing up in a world in which all traditional categories are being blurred and all institutions questioned – a characteristic of postmodernism.[10]

WHY WRITE A BOOK ON MUSIC TELEVISION?

In one sense, my writing a book on MTV requires no explanation: I have long been interested in popular culture, focusing particularly on the classical Hollywood film but also on women's popular fiction and commercial television. And MTV, as a new popular phenomenon, would seem to warrant study as much as anything else.

However, as it is many years since I last studied adolescent or youth culture, a few words of explanation may be in order. I first became interested in youth culture when teaching in a further education college in London in the early 1960s. At that time, of course, there was not much youth culture proper, this being prior to the explosion of the Beatles and the proliferation of a very clearly defined adolescent and young adult group whose various cultural innovations and political activities would become news headlines for more than a decade.

Bobby Duran, Adam Faith, and Cliff Richard (sometimes seen as a tame British Elvis Presley) more or less represented the music interests of our students in those days. Well-dressed, clean, and conservative, these rock singers did not represent much of a rebellion to the status quo. The Teddy Boys alone, with their well-oiled hair and suits modeled on Edwardian dress, suggested any oppositional culture. We had in all this only a glimpse of the mid 1960s and 1970s youth culture explosion, in which rock and roll was to play a central, often subversive, role that has been well-documented.[11]

At Kingsway Day College, London, following the approach worked out by Paddy Whannel and Stuart Hall, we tried to indicate the disparities between the trivialized experiences of this early British pop music and commercial film, and the more complex possibilities of what we still called "great art."[12] But this was carried out with enormous respect for the commercial works our students were drawn to, and usually involved understanding, and helping them understand, the bases for their interests rather than attempting to turn them toward the canon. Mostly we tried to interest them in the new working-class culture of the period, represented by the plays of Arnold Wesker, John Osborne, and John Arden; the novels of Alan Sillitoe, David Storey, and John Braine; and the films often made out of these novels by Tony Richardson, Lindsay Anderson, John Schlesinger, and Karel Reisz.

However, this lesson in realism was rather bleak and humorless, just like the works themselves. Only so much could be said about the banal, boring working-class lives of the protagonists, and texts did not seem to offer a way out. No wonder the British Youth responded with glee to the Beatles, who finally introduced joy/exuberance/fun into the traumatized post-World-War-II British landscape. But by then I had left England.

It is a far cry from the early steps toward a youth culture in Britain briefly sketched in here to the full-blown, heavily commercialized youth phenomenon that MTV represents. In the 1960s I was part of the politicized youth culture, although we all kept up with the Hippies, the Flower Children, and the rock and roll culture, especially as represented by the Beatles, the Stones, the Grateful Dead, the Doors, Led Zeppelin, Janis Joplin. But in the 1970s I dropped out to become an adult, only vaguely keeping track of punk, new wave and heavy metal – largely through my daughter.

Obviously these "developments" partly paved the way for MTV. Perhaps the subject attracts me because it contains remnants from the first ten years of the youth culture that I had known, together with the less familiar – to me – 1970s. But MTV also attracts because it seems to embody aspects of contemporary youth culture that signify a new era. It attracts, that is, by its very combination of similarity to, and *difference* from, my own various youth cultures; and by seeming to be an index of a new stage of things, a different kind of consciousness. I will be suggesting what this new consciousness involves, using postmodernism and psychoanalysis to illuminate it. More than much previous popular culture, MTV makes evident its address to adolescent desire, to the spectator's imaginary repertoire, which now takes precedence over any obvious political stance toward dominant culture. Obsessed like much popular culture has always been with sexuality and violence, rock videos nevertheless represent these in new ways.

This new consciousness is perhaps partly the result of the Cold War, nuclear technology, multinational corporate capitalisms, star wars, advanced computer and other high tech developments, as well as, on a more mundane level, being produced by highly sophisticated new marketing strategies, building upon ever-increasing knowledge of psychological manipulation. In other words, MTV seems to embody what Jameson and others have been calling *Postmodernism*.

I am concerned with postmodernism on a number of different levels. The first level, already briefly touched on but to be fully developed later, presents the televisual apparatus as itself postmodernist, with MTV carrying this characteristic to an extreme; second is the more strictly aesthetic level, to be addressed in Chapter 3, where the technical, formal strategies of MTV videos are seen to generally embody postmodernism; third is the postmodernist "ideology" or "world view" as it emerges from in-depth analysis of specific videos, a project to be undertaken in Chapters 4 and 5.

The effort to find a label to indicate a new stage of things in itself reflects the nature of the crisis. People of older generations sense that the old categories will no longer serve, and yet can do no better than to come up with a term that includes the prefix "post" attached to what was a familiar category, namely "modernism."[13] By this strategy, one hopes to indicate a connection with what was, with the familiar, while at the same time noting the difference, the new, the unknowable.

Now MTV obviously is connected with past developments, as my analysis will reveal. But that connection may not quite be what the "post" prefix suggests: that is, what is important is the sort of use made of the past by contemporary youth culture rather than *the fact that* the past is used. The manner of use suggests a drastically Other consciousness for which a completely new word may well be better than "postmodernism." But we have not yet made a sufficiently clear break with the past, nor with the concept of historical evolution, to arrive at a new word. And for my purposes, the notion of the postmodern is helpful in providing a method of conceptualizing what is *different* about the new phase. One cannot think without a shaping framework: it seems to me that the only way to understand a new phenomenon must be through understanding why one's current categories do not fit. Working dialectically, then, we can move beyond current categories to new ones in a way impossible without *moving through* the old ones.

Clearly, since each generation enters the stream at a different point, the same phenomenon will take a different shape if studied by people with different starting frameworks. Someone looking at MTV from the position of growing up in the 1970s is bound to bring to it frameworks other than mine, and come up with different results. Indeed, someone like Greil Marcus might argue that I cannot possibly write about MTV since I did not grow up with it, and have not belonged in a network of teenagers who "lived" rock music daily, and for whom this was a silent common bond.[14]

I do not agree with the notion of rock music as a kind of mystique that someone outside the specific generation cannot understand. But reading Marcus made me aware of how different MTV is from previous rock cultures in terms of its address. For Marcus, 1960s rock was something that bound his small circle together in a largely non-verbal way; they shared the common, secret bond of enjoying the same songs, all of which represented a certain stance toward the establishment, a shared set of mildly subversive values. This is something that I will be exploring later, so let me merely note here that the very fact that MTV addresses itself to a broad, generally youthful section of the American public that ranges from 12 to 34 on up distinguishes it from earlier rock cultures, which addressed

8

much more homogeneous groups, clearly defined in terms of values, age, and social status.

But the point about looking at MTV from different conceptual frameworks raises a problem that confronted me in setting out on my project, that is, what use to make of rock history in my text. As will be clear in a later chapter, MTV situates itself in a special way vis-à-vis past rock movements, and must be positioned outside of what has become a familiar linear history of rock developments.

Like most history, that of rock music has now developed its own narrative pattern, repeated from text to text. One of the earliest histories was Nick Cohn's *Rock From the Beginning* (1969), whose basic linear model has been taken up by later histories (such as Jahn's *From Elvis Presley to the Rolling Stones*).[15] Let me briefly rehearse this narrative, if only to indicate a historical sequence that now seems to have run its course. By this I mean that trends set in motion originally by black musicians have possibly gone as far as they can, as is arguably the case with modern art developments. Part of what we call the postmodern is precisely this phase of a movement that seems to have reached the end of its line.

MTV arguably emerges at this historical moment just because such an impasse in popular rock music has been reached. The historical "line" goes pretty much as follows: Everyone sees the 1950s as the great founding moment of rock music, which has its origins in black Rhythm and Blues, and in the Country and Western music that itself drew heavily on black music. Most historians comment on the way that white imitations of black songs were acceptable whereas the black originals were not. Billy Haley and Elvis Presley are central to everyone's story as setting the stage for all that happened subsequently. Presley, with his extraordinary mixture of pop and blues, foreshadows later rock developments. Early 1960s rock is viewed as a product of both Rhythm and Blues and of 1950s rock: the Beatles are credited with revolutionizing sound with their new instruments, new combinations, and new use of Indian forms and musical themes.

Historians vary somewhat in the degree to which they see late 1960s so-called "acid" or "protest" rock as innovative; most agree that the "hippie" music did introduce new sounds and new instruments, and that the advances possible through new musical technology (especially the capacity to increase volume) did have a big impact. Most writers agree, too, that this period represents the high point in recent rock history, and honor the original contributions of the Rolling Stones, the Beatles, the Who, Led Zeppelin, and the Kinks (among others) from Britain; and of Bob Dylan, the Grateful Dead, Janis Joplin, Jimi Hendrix, the Doors, and the Jefferson Airplane, from America. The important "protest" element is generally agreed upon, although the actual political significance of the stances taken by late 1960s rock musicians in their lives and lyrics is debated.

The narrative generally sees the 1970s as representing a decline in American rock, which had led the way in the late 1960s. Continuing the story of mutual back-and-forth influencing between England and America, historians now see the British moving in to fill the gap with their new wave and punk rock bands that gradually revitalized the American scene in the mid 1970s. Punk and new wave took on a different tone and style in America: already well on their way to postmodernism, it took the peculiar nature of the 1980s political scene in America to move the trends over into a full-blown postmodernism.

In this recurrent "dialogue" between America and Britain, MTV may be America's latest contribution. If postmodernism really does herald a new era, requiring totally new historical and aesthetic paradigms, it may signal the end of the kind of historical processes that rock history texts describe. That is, we may no longer be looking for "pendulum" swings but for something else.

Whether or not MTV can be considered as in the mainstream of rock history, or an altogether different development, it seems necessary to link it, however tenuously, with the past.[16] I will argue that rock and pop forms from the past thirty years or so are currently being used to express a new sensibility that has been labeled "postmodernist." As we'll see, MTV uses themes, motifs, and forms from rock and pop history indiscriminately and without recognizing what it is doing, or making distinctions between rock "proper" and its popularized forms.[17] It cannot therefore be said either to represent a reaction to what went before or to foreshadow what will come hereafter. It is precisely those sorts of linear progressions that it violates in not situating itself within their parameters.

INTRODUCTION

Let me remind readers that this book addresses itself not to rock videos in general but to their incorporation in the institution that is MTV. Rock videos have their own history as an art form (a history being documented as of writing in an unprecedented Museum of Modern Art exhibition),[18] and are exhibited in a variety of different contexts. In most European countries there is no 24-hour channel like MTV devoted to videos; there, videos have half-hour slots on the different channels, a kind of visual "Top of the Pops." Often there are merely short clips from the videos in the count-down. Videos can be seen on a home VCR, since the cassettes are available, but one usually has to rent an entire tape by one artist. While the individual analyses of rock videos in this book should be interesting, my argument about rock videos and postmodernism depends on their exhibition in the 24-hour, continuous context.

Much of MTV's particular institutional form can be accounted for by looking at its links to a mode that at first seems to be the antithesis of rock music, namely advertising. It is to the wedding of rock music and aesthetic visual forms drawn partly from advertising that I now turn.

1

MTV: advertising and production

It was the sometimes extraordinary and innovative avant-garde techniques that first drew the attention of the critical establishment to MTV. It was tempting to view these devices as serving similar functions to those they served in what is now "traditional" modernism; but as we'll see in the next chapter, this is not so. In any case, the devices masked the promotional and commercial aspects of MTV that are evident in the contexts of production and exhibition.

But before I discuss the similarities between rock videos and ads, as specific texts, let me note how in its overall, 24-hour flow, MTV functions like one continuous ad in that nearly all of its short segments are indeed ads of one kind or another. If it is true that commercials constitute the *real* TV dramas in the case of series programs like soaps[1] then how much more true is this of a channel like Music Television that contains little else *but* ads of various kinds. As I'll show toward the end of this chapter, the various ad-segments, whether they be rock videos, a Levi or Cooler commercial, or promos for MTV itself, all have come to look more and more alike. It is for this reason that MTV, more than other television, may be said to be *about* consumption. It evokes a kind of hypnotic trance in which the spectator is suspended in a state of unsatisfied desire but forever under the illusion of *imminent* satisfaction through some kind of purchase. This desire is displaced onto the record that will embody the star's magnetism and fascination.

ADVERTISING AND PRODUCTION

The rock video idea was originally an advertising idea; in fact, a better name for rock videos is really "rock promos," since they are widely seen as promotional tools for the record companies.[2] The word "promo" is also appropriate because it indicates the videos' links to advertising evident in their style and manner of production. Their short, four-minute span originally suited a promotional context, while the illogical image-change and generally "avant-garde" techniques mimicked those long customary in many ads. The reliance on freelance crews, the omission of production credits and the financial tie-in to the record companies all duplicate the production situation of ads.

Interestingly, the promotional videos, which have hitherto been provided free by the record companies on the model of companies giving radio stations free records, are now in competition with one another for space on the channel. In the near future, record companies may have to pay to have videos on MTV. Given the already considerable cost of producing a video (from $35,000 to $50,000 at least), which is usually shouldered by the record company, this would be taxing. Several directors in a *Variety* interview suggested that record companies would be happy to be rid of the need to produce videos, for which they have "no clear-cut recoupment." Others, however, pointed out MTV's function in promoting songs not on the radio charts and in keeping songs in circulation that would otherwise have died. All seemed to agree, however, that a good video could not make a smash out of a "mediocre" song.[3] The huge success of Jackson's "Thriller" evidently convinced record companies of what videos could do, and interested several of them in the longer format (but so far as I can see, only David Bowie has taken advantage of extra time).

Exactly how any particular video was produced (who financed it, what artists were involved) is unclear to the viewer, since no credits of any kind are given (the rock group, the title of the song, and the record it comes from are the only clues). Full credits are given only for each week's video that is Top of the Countdown, and for those that make it to the MTV Awards ceremony. Directors differ greatly in the degree to which they demand or receive artistic freedom, though undoubtedly some see a tension between the record companies and themselves which is exacerbated by the fact that the companies are responsible for the financing.[4]

13

Rock videos differ from ads in the degree of concern for artistic elements. In this sense they are a hybrid form, in between the ad and the pop culture text. Directors themselves are a mixed bunch, drawn from a variety of backgrounds. Those coming from commercials think about a video very differently from those coming from independent filmmaking. Ken Walz is concerned that videos are becoming increasingly commercial, with record companies demanding "a more scientific approach to writing, producing and directing . . . videos." He fears that the more commercial directors get into the scene, the more they will feel comfortable with such restrictions and the less creativity there will be.[5] Other directors in the group interviewed have not yet felt the restrictions of commercials and apparently see themselves free to create what they want. All agree that there is often tension among the three main groups involved in production – the performers, the artists, and the record company. Directors believe they are the ones who know what has to be done and who can best come up with suitable ideas, but often performers or company people think they know best. Some directors find the record companies at a loss because the rock video is such a new form, and only too glad to leave things up to the person they have hired. The possibility for creativity in music video production is evident in the big name film directors (Brian de Palma and John Sayles have already made videos) now becoming interested in making videos just because of the greater freedom than Hollywood that videos offer.

An important problem mentioned by the directors interviewed is that usually the song is written first, and therefore takes priority over the visuals, limiting visual possibilities. The creativity of the film director has to be subordinated to that of the song-writer and performer. One director suggested that a rock star should begin working with a director at the point of conceptualizing the song but this is clearly impractical.[6] Others are concerned that videos may begin to affect the music negatively. August Darnell, organizer and chief composer for a band (Kid Creole and the Coconuts), is quoted as saying that "The attention that used to be devoted to content and song form is now being given over to the videos."[7] How things are finally resolved in the current set-up varies from case to case.

A second source of conflict is that between the groups producing the video (usually the director and the performers) and MTV as an

14

institution. Because videos are more than *merely* ads (they are, as it were, ads plus), artists and bands have already, in MTV's short history, been in conflict with MTV management and with the record companies. There is a built-in contradiction, familiar from Hollywood, between the interests of the artists and performers and of those creating a profitable enterprise. In a predictable cycle, the more tapes were adapted to what would please the largest audience, the more successful the channel, and the greater the urge to censor material. Wary both of parental objections to the cable and of white audiences in racist parts of America, MTV at first censored black bands and explicit sex (e.g. Frankie Goes to Hollywood's *Relax*).

The motivations for both kinds of censorship were probably mainly commercial, but Dr York, one of the American black artists who has had trouble getting videos shown on MTV, is convinced that it is the difficulty of finding sponsors for the channel when black artists are featured that has kept them off MTV. According to Dr York, advertising strategists find the market for blacks hard to predict and unreliable, and thus are wary of committing money for promoting the music of black artists.[8]

As a result of objections raised by well-known stars like David Bowie, who refused to have videos on MTV if the situation continued, things improved somewhat in 1984 – 5. Predictably, changes have been merely in line with what the establishment could tolerate; that is, videos by black artists like Prince and Michael Jackson who have obviously "made it" are played from time to time, but black bands are still by far in the minority in the regular MTV run.[9] Prince is featured regularly only when he has a hit (like "Purple Rain" or "Raspberry Beret"), but was rarely represented until his recent, mildly scandalous "Kiss" video that (perhaps because of its explicit sexuality) did not remain long in circulation. Now that Michael Jackson is out of the news, his videos are also only rarely seen. Until the recent advent of Whitney Houston, Tina Turner was the only female black singer featured regularly, and even so, her videos are few and far between. Aretha Franklin's "Freeway of Love" was played frequently when it got into the top twenty, but we have mainly seen her since then co-starring with white artists (see below); the Pointer Sisters' "Neutron Dance" was only their second video since "Jump" to be shown, and their newest video appeared only recently. Black artists who are not well known cannot get a video on MTV in the way that a similarly obscure white rock musician can, and rightly feel discriminated against by the channel; they have to content themselves with appearances on the weekly programs on other channels already mentioned, or on cable slots.

As of writing, one solution for black artists who want to get on MTV is to make videos jointly with white artists. Phil Collins and Phil Bailey paved the way with their successful "Easy Lover," and the video perhaps still represents the most playful and thoroughly integrated of joint videos. Hall and Oates made a successful video with David Ruffin and Eddie Kendrick, played constantly in September 1985. Most recently, Robin Clark has appeared with Simple Minds in their successful "Alive and Kicking" (top of the countdown for several weeks in 1986), and again in their "All The Things She Said" (she is apparently becoming a staple of their act); Aretha Franklin is given homage in Whitney Houston's "How Will I Know", but appears most dramatically with Annie Lennox in their powerful "Sisters Are Doin' It For Themselves", discussed in Chapter 5.

The other use of black artists – namely as back up choir and/or dancing figures (as in Young's "Everytime You Go Away" or Sting's successful "If You Love Somebody, Set Them Free") still seems somewhat exploitative, but perhaps better than nothing. The September 1985 MTV Video Awards broke new ground in having Eddie Murphy as the host and including more black artists than ever before. Perhaps because of this, in combination with the space that Channel Three has been providing especially for black artists (in the Video Soul and Video Vibrations slots), in Summer 1986 lesser known black artists, often relying on rap and reggae music that MTV has hitherto claimed was not their province,[10] appeared more frequently. A striking example of this is the recent success of the rap group Run – DMC's "Walk This Way," which has been in the countdown several times and has been frequently cycled on the channel. This success will no doubt pave the way for more rap groups, such as Whodini, to get on MTV. Janet and Jermaine Jackson, possibly because of their famous connection, and Jermaine Stewart, are currently paving the way for others.

Censorship of sex seems to be relaxing, but again this is a mixed blessing. Homosexuality is not addressed directly (I will be discussing

16

bi-sexuality and androgyny in their constricted forms later on), and relaxing of sex censorship has merely permitted degrading images of the female body (not that dissimilar from some pornography) to emerge (see John Cougar's "Hurts So Good," etc. discussed in Chapter 5, Prince's "1999," or his recent "Kiss" video mentioned above). Some of the most sexist heavy metal bands, such as Ozzy Osbourne, Motley Crue, Judas Priest, Alice Cooper, and Twisted Sister, have recently become popular and are now featured on MTV regularly (heavy metal bands were earlier censored), particularly in the weekly "Most Requested Videos" slot. (As of writing, there is a special "Heavy Metal" slot on the channel, presumably as a result of popular demand.) Twisted Sister's extraordinary video "Leader of the Pack" details, in comic mode, the incredibly violent adventures of a proper middle-class girl en route to union with one of the awesomely endowed band members parading huge biceps, broad chest, and hair down to the waist. Ozzy Osbourne's "Shot in the Dark" similarly shows the transformation of another middle-class girl into a zebra-like seductress through Osbourne's initiation rites; while Alice Cooper's "(He's Back): He's the Man Behind the Mask" this time has a middle-class young *male* terrifyingly inducted into the Alice Cooper nether world.

Artists and performers are naturally implicated in the contradictions because the increased success of the channel means their increased exposure and sales. They cannot help being involved because of their status as mediatory objects between a private and a public sphere. The artists' subjectivity is constructed for them through their involvement in the public sphere, changing their relationship to society. Although personally they may object to racism, since their success depends on exposure on MTV they are brought to acquiesce.

Here the similarity between ads and videos is central, for, as Stephen Levy notes, "MTV's greatest achievement has been to coax rock and roll into the video arena where you can't distinguish between entertainment and the sales pitch."[11] The "sales pitch" has two objects, first that of selling the MTV station itself, second that of selling the band and their song/album. In both cases, videos function like advertising, in which the signifier that addresses desire is linked to a commodity. The signifiers used to sell the MTV station address the desire for (1) power and virility, and (2) nurturance and community, neatly combining appeals to both male and female spectators. Power and virility (and, one might suggest, patriotism) are signified by the huge rocket plunging into outer space, followed by images of men on the moon exploring new territory. (Interestingly, this logo has remained constant since MTV's inception, attesting presumably to its expression of an appeal basic to the channel.) Another logo, now dropped, used to show a TV monitor, scrawled with the letters MTV, into which a globe dropped (MTV *is* the world!), but has been replaced with logos insisting that, with its 24-hour flow, MTV is LIFE!, and with an image of a gleaming, stream-lined subway train coming to a halt. The idea is clear: MTV equals the men exploring outer space in its breaking of new territory, and also equals new technologies, the future. MTV claims also to encompass all that the young adult needs – it is the World as well as Life. One logo references the Aztec culture, showing its monuments being toppled over. MTV is a "civilization" greater than the Aztec.

Interestingly enough, in 1986, an MTV logo began to reflect the various debates about MTV and rock videos generally (like, for instance, those started by the parents against rock (PMRC) organization). The logo cleverly seeks to co-opt objections by satirizing them: one logo shows a man watching MTV for 24-hours, taking its own ad literally; he becomes increasingly dishevelled and ill, until a voice-over says that MTV is *bad* for you. Another logo consists of interviews with people describing the evil things that go on on MTV; the *appeal* now is to the illicit, but it is in fact obvious that all is quite innocent.[12]

There used to be a vivid signifier for nurturance, namely the plaintive, child-like voice of Pete Townshend or Mick Jagger (both attentive early on to the possibilities of MTV) saying "I want my MTV!" (i.e. "I want my Mommy, my milk"), but this is no longer played. The station now relies on its trusty veejays (Martha Quinn, Mark Goodman, Alan Hunter, and J.J. Jackson) to create an appeal essential for the success of the station, that is the creation of a casual, intimate ambience. (In 1986, some new veejays (like Chuck Slick Kanter) were added, and older ones phased out or given less time.) After intensive marketing research, Robert Pittman hit upon the desire for a pseudo, rock and roll "family," very much along the lines of that deliberately created in programs like *Good Morning America* to appeal to adults.[13] But in this case, the "family" was to be a family of peers, very deliberately lacking adults. The supposedly informal, easy, and relaxed style of the veejays was intended to conjure up the natural ambience of teenagers gathered in a room to listen to music with their peers. (My sophisticated sources tell me that the ambience is far from being convincingly "natural," seeming rather deliberately fake to these viewers, and indeed MTV is all pre-recorded.[14] They resent the forced attempt to be one with the audience.[15]) The decision not to include any news except that relating to music further ensured the absence of adult authority figures. MTV thus constructs a false sense of addressing a unified teenage rock "community," fulfilling young people's desire to belong in a world without parents.

But in addition to selling itself, MTV also sells the music and the bands featured in videos. Here the signifiers that address desire (for sex, violence, freedom, love) are fastened onto the commodity that is, in this case, the band and their music contained in the purchasable album. The desire is displaced onto the album, which then promises to satisfy it, in the familiar manner of advertisements.

Videos differ in the degree to which they feature the rock star in performance and other members of the band playing their various instruments. But those that do clearly show traces of the tapes of live performances that preceded MTV, and of live transmissions. Performers and managers here rely on the star phenomenon, promoting an identification with band members that will bring teenagers out to live concerts and persuade them to buy not only albums but also all the paraphernalia (T-shirts, jackets, hats, etc.) related to the stars. (Interestingly, the directors in the *Variety* interview by and large thought performance videos boring, and were annoyed by the insistence of performers and record companies on the stars being seen in the videos. Several would have preferred to make videos entirely without featuring the stars, but the hard-sell aspect demands their presence.) The 1985 ad for a look-alike Michael Jackson coat shows the way that the phenomenon can be capitalized on by firms outside of the record companies and band managers and, as of writing, a big selling campaign for look-alike Madonna "Susan" jackets is underway. The recent look-alike rock star contests (in which teenagers compete for the best imitation in synch sound of a rock star's look, performance-style,

19

dress, and movements) encourage teenager identification with the stars, increasing their dedicated close listening to, and watching of, the stars' voices, actions, movements, and clothes. The gimmick is yet one more piece of evidence for the centrality of advertising to the whole MTV institution and mode of operation.

At first, MTV was watched mainly by young people within the privacy of their homes. Many teenagers report concentrated watching as a relaxation, particularly if they do not have cable and see MTV at a friend's house. The experience is then often a group one, people responding loudly to their likes and dislikes as part of the fun. Often, however, the program provides the background for casual partying rather than being watched concentratedly by teenagers. While some teenagers report watching the program alone, many evidently use it as background music (not attending to the visuals) while doing homework, much as they would use the radio.[16] Others match the visuals to music they prefer.

The visual dimension, however, obviously sets certain constraints upon sites of consumption. (Given the current stage of technology, people could, but do not yet, carry around small TV sets as they do small radios since the cost is prohibitive. The Walkman phenomenon, moreover, allows people to *listen* to music in many more contexts than they can *look* at videos.) But still MTV is "consumed" in a variety of settings, ranging from the lounge or cafeteria of the college student center (where MTV may be either piped in live or students operate a pay-per-video machine), to the dance club scene in cities – where TV screens dot the various floors above and behind the dancers, to the large department store where the TV set playing MTV may be seen in the youth clothes sections.

MTV, then, exists in a variety of sites of reception, although the home is still presumably the largest. The channel consists of a variety of things, including the veejay's comments and introductions to videos, their specific Music News and Concert Tour Information sections, their advertising of MTV promotional items like T-shirts, and their interviews with various stars, usually pre-taped. There are also music competitions, winners getting prizes such as a weekend with one of the rock stars or a flight to London and a screen appearance, or a rock star's special car. There are weekly events, such as The Friday Night Video Fights, the Saturday Night Countdown, the

ADVERTISING AND PRODUCTION

MTV Feature Event (consisting, in Spring 1986, of skits by the Monkees), or the late night weekend live concerts.

Interspersed with all this material are the ads by companies sponsoring the station. Usually in groups of four at a stretch, these are predictably geared to the young adult audience, and are increasingly themselves extremely short rock videos. This is so much the case that the uninitiated viewer cannot at first tell whether a TV-segment is going to be an ad or a rock video.

According to random sample hours documented in June 1985, the proportion of videos to other material is now almost half.[17] This proportion may vary at different times in the 24-hour flow, but the point is that there is significantly more promotional material other than regular ads and the videos than when MTV started in 1981 – a fact that attests to the increasing commercialization of the channel as it has succeeded. At the end of 1986, MTV began to imitate radio rock stations in their new "four in a row" strategy, which cuts into ad time in those 30-minute sections. It is the mechanism of identification which advertising relies on, and which is central in MTV videos, that I want now to discuss.

2

History, "reading formations," and the televisual apparatus in MTV

At the end of the last chapter, I began to address the issue of spectator identification with MTV rock stars as encouraged by the station's management in order to involve teenagers even more with the channel, and thus increase consumption. But the issue of identification raises all the larger ones about the way any individual (i.e. historical subject) receives a popular text; this involves the codes that govern such a spectator, and affect response, making him/her receptive to appeals like that of the "look-alike" contests (to be discussed later on). The related issue of the kind of spectator positions that MTV videos construct or, perhaps better, *offer*, will be dealt with in a later chapter. But both issues involve attention to the specifically *televisual* (as against filmic) apparatus, since both the historical and hypothetical or model spectator (the latter "constructed" through textual strategies) are differently positioned in television from in film.

Here I want to deal with the *historical* televisual spectator, and it may be useful to set up the discussion by briefly summarizing theoretical positions as they have been developed in relation to film. In the early 1970s, contemporary film theory replaced the old notion of history as the "truth of past experience and the truth of present accounts of it"[1] with two main concepts, influenced by semiology and psychoanalysis, that located history in the register of signifying practices. In other words, the notion that "To learn lessons from the past, it is necessary only to unlock this truth"[2] was shown to be invalid in the light of new understandings about the way discourses, past and present, function.

First, Emile Benveniste's distinction between history and discourse represented a major influence in reconceptualizing the old notions of history as truth.[3] Christian Metz used Benveniste's categories to distinguish the classical realist Hollywood film from the avant-garde text. History, as a concept, was removed from the terrain of knowledge about social events to that of "fiction," analagous to any classic text. History and the classical film were alike in being present to the reader/spectator, "but only as something which is already past and which has already a fixed resolution for the problem it evokes."[4] Or, in Metz's words, "The 'story' as system makes it possible to reconcile all, since history, in Benveniste's terms, is always (by definition) a story told from nowhere, told by nobody but received by someone (without which it could not exist)."[5] Discourse, on the other hand, in foregrounding the source of enunciation suppressed in history, describes the avant-garde address, always eager to comment on its own processes.

The second set of concepts that located history in the register of signifying practices rather than of ontological "truth" was initiated by Foucault, who used a very different notion of discourse in looking at power as displayed through institutions. For Foucault, history became the study of discursive practices, which, like texts, function to construct and position subjects in their lived experiences. That is, people's daily lives are shaped and governed by institutional discourses outside of their control, which the historian can rediscover by looking at documents (that contain the discourses) as evidence. Foucault's work was important in combining Althusserian Marxism with Lacanian ideas about the constitution of the subject through language, so as to theorize the subject in history.[6] Against the project of a "continuous history," with its "indispensable correlative of the founding function of the subject," Foucault proposes "An enterprise by which one tries to measure the mutations that operate in general in the field of history . . . an enterprise by which one tries to throw off the last anthropological constraints; an enterprise that wishes, in return, to reveal how these constraints could come about."[7]

23

Under similar intellectual influences, Roland Barthes shifted the emphasis from the *text's* strategies, that had preoccupied semiologists like Umberto Eco, to the function of the subject in creating the text. But, if the text cannot exist without the subject, the subject, for Barthes, also cannot exist without the text. As he put it, "The reader is the space on which all the quotations that make up a writing are inscribed without any of them being lost; a text's unity lies not in its origin but in its destination . . . (The reader) is simply that someone who holds together in a single field all the traces by which the written text is constituted."[8] Metz developed similar notions in relation specifically to the film, noting that "In watching the film, I help it to be born, I help it to live, since it is in me that it will live and it was made for that, to be seen, i.e. to come into existence only when it is seen."[9] The subject is thus as much constructed in the process of reading a text as, in the Lacanian model, it is constructed in the process of the entry into language and the symbolic.

As a result of these theories, the historical subject was written out of film theory, first because we could know nothing about any such subject, and second because the subject was in any case fixed into the position constructed for him/her by the institutional practices or the filmic/literary text. Neither Foucault nor Barthes were interested in the empirical level of things: Foucault, for instance, did not try to find out how far any actual historical subjects resisted the positioning that institutional discourses constructed for them. Feminist historians, on the other hand, often provide information about women that shows their local resistance to dominant discourses; only then these positivist historians have not researched the resistance in terms of over-arching institutional discourses, or shown any interest in the complexities of subject construction. It seems to me that ideally we need historians able to work on both fronts at once.

In relation to literary and film texts, both certain Marxists and feminists have objected to the way that the historical subject has been all but written out of critical discourse. The few empirical studies that existed (such as David Morley's on the British TV program *Nationwide*)[10] were marginalized, suspect because the information could only be "subjective impressions," of no general or scientific value. The common objection has been that the theories sketched in above constructed a monolithic, a-historical spectator, not distinguished in terms of race, class, gender or *context* of reception.[11] A further objection is that the spectator has also not been differentiated in terms of historical *time*, i.e. the time of the text's production and original exhibition, and the time of the subject receiving it. The codes governing the historical subject in each case will be different, and thus the "reading" of the text will have to be different.

Stephen Heath, always mindful of the historical subject and of the issues in relation to him/her, is important in initiating corrective work, but seems ultimately to return to a position whereby the historical subject is unable to resist textual construction. In his important essay, "Film performance," Heath begins by recognizing the historical subject.[12] He notes that while "the individual is always a subject in society, the place of social and ideological formations," he/she is always more than simply "the figure of that representation, is in excess of such placing formations" (p. 126). He goes on to note that the crucial element of ideological systems is "the number of machines (institutions) that can *move* the individual as subject, shifting and tying desire, realigning excess and contradiction, in a perpetual retotalization – a remembering – of the imaginary in which the individual subject is grasped as identity" (p. 127). Heath here, and in the following discussion, seems to elide the historical subject, that he *does* recognize, with the subject constructed through representations, through what he calls the "novelistic" process. For Heath, cinema "occupies the individual as subject in the terms of the existing social representations and it constructs the individual as subject in the process, in the balancing out of symbolic and imaginary, circulation for fixity" (p. 127). Heath does not allow for the possibility of two conflicting subject constructions; rather, he sees cinema as an institution *completing* the subject, as "the translation of plurality into a *certain* history, the single vision" (p. 128). Like Barthes, then, Heath ultimately sees the fictive text as necessarily constructing the subject in the processes of reception. As he puts it, "What moves in film, finally, is the spectator, immobile in front of the screen. Film is the regulation of that movement, the individual as subject held in the shifting and placing of desire, energy, contradiction . . . The spectator is *moved* and *related* as subject in the process and images of that movement."

Recent Marxist theorists like Tony Bennett and Keith Tribe, and various film historians like Robert Allen, Janet Staiger, David Bordwell, and Kristin Thompson, have begun to address the problem regarding the historical subject as outlined in the above theories.[13] Bennett has usefully attempted to differentiate theoretically the hypothetical or model spectator that texts construct or offer (and this is an important distinction) from the historical subject. Building on the work of Ernesto Laclau and Michel Pêcheux,[14] together, perhaps, with that of Marxist Formalist Eikenbaum, Bennett argues that the relationship is best conceived of as dialectical. According to Ron Levaco, this was a perception already to be found in embryo in Eikenbaum's work. As Levaco, summarizing Eikenbaum, puts it:

> From this Marxist viewpoint, what is important is that while the text of any artwork may appear patently static, it must be understood that its meaning is dialectical, a reciprocal expression of society and culture, situated and understood by auditors at a particular moment in history. . . . And that the events of history and the advances of technology can and do transform the signification of the artwork for any human subject situated in history.[15]

Bennett's theory allows, not for *individual impressions* as unique experiences relying on some essential subject, but rather for the subject's coming to the text with already coded perceptions of the world that he calls "reading formations":

> By reading formations, I mean a set of discursive and intertextual determinations which organize and animate the practice of reading, connecting texts and readers in specific relations to one another in constituting reading subjects of particular types and texts as objects to be read in particular ways.[16]

An individual's reading formations may have been shaped either by the same dominant codes as govern the popular text being read/ viewed, in which case there will be no tension; or by some sub-culture – such as feminism, trades unionism, Marxism, Moral Majority thinking, homosexuality, identification with minorities, etc. – in which case the spectator may refuse the offered position, resist the positioning he/she is experiencing. With a popular text made at an historical time different from that of the spectator, there may be, as Eikenbaum already saw, an ideological discrepancy, such as around race or gender.

Keith Tribe, meanwhile, usefully distinguished an *anti-history* position from an *anti-historicist* one. He argued that "history" is something perpetually constructed in a specific conjuncture and that it is necessary always to question historical discourse about the arguments it supports, about what it does. History is always the result, not of a revelation of the past, but of "determinate relations in a given conjuncture."[17] But many have been limited by the psychoanalytic paradigm to a focus on the a-historical psychic mechanisms that position the spectator. Building on Laura Mulvey's pioneering essay,[18] feminist theorists have been exploring the complexity of what it means to be a female spectator, but have tended to ignore the issue of *historicizing* that spectator.

Her focus on narrative has, however, recently led Teresa de Lauretis to insert the female historical spectator. De Lauretis argues that theorists have ignored, in favor of gaze-image dichotomies, a second set of identifications involving identification with the "figure of narrative movement, the mythical subject, and with the figure of narrative closure, the narrative image." This leaves room for "a double female desire (for the Father and for the Mother)" that will be useful in understanding gender address in some MTV.[19]

Nevertheless, although De Lauretis does insert the historical spectator, her theory still assumes, in accord with the psychoanalytic paradigm, a female spectator undifferentiated in terms of race, class or reading formations. Just because it is a special kind of art form, as we've already seen, involving different kinds of gender address, a 24-hour continuous flow, song-image format, MTV is a useful terrain on which to explore issues about history, the historical spectator, and gender. I will address the specificities of gender address in Chapter 5, but want here to deal more generally with two issues: first, how far even the modified theories developed in relation to film (i.e. the distinction between a model and a historical spectator) apply to the different televisual apparatus; and second, the degree to which MTV may be seen once again to embody in extreme form what is inherent to television generally.

27

Regarding the first question, does a similar distinction between a model and a historical spectator arise in the television situation? The distinction certainly makes some sense given the filmic apparatus, although once we make the comparison to television, one realizes the far greater *textual* construction of the spectator in film. What Heath says about the spectator, "immobile in front of the screen," ultimately being all that moves in film ("moved and related as subject in the process and images of that movement") highlights the different relationship of the TV spectator to the screen. While we saw the necessity to point out the existence of the historical film spectator, that spectator is usually overwhelmed by his/her textual construction.

The relationship between the historical and model spectators in television is different on both sides of the screen, as it were. For the spectator is not as monolithically constructed, as a result of the fragmentation of the viewing experience; but he/she is paradoxically also less the separate historical spectator as well. While the film spectator is drawn into the filmic world through structures that appear to satisfy the desire for plenitude and for the unification of split subjectivity, the TV spectator is drawn into the TV world through the mechanism of consumption (i.e. constant unsatisfied desire, the constant hope of a forthcoming but never realized plenitude). It is the endlessness of the series of TV texts – a continuous strip, as noted, that is always available to the spectator even when the set is off – that produces this different effect. For the subject is always a potential viewer at the flick of the switch, as is not the case for the film spectator, who pays for and consumes a delimited "text" in a fixed space and amount of time.

This means that the TV world is more like the actual world of the TV viewer in that it goes on and on, 24 hours a day, and is always "available." The historical spectator is more inside the TV world than is the film spectator who knows that he is "dreaming." The distinction between "fiction" and "reality" is less obvious to the TV spectator just because, as Robert Stam has argued, the *reality-effect* is greater and the regression to the dream state far less.[20] There is thus less *cause* for the historical spectator to resist his/her textual construction since the relationship relies less on that kind of construction than on the *simulation* of an *object-relationship,* of a kind of one-on-one intimacy that Jane Feuer and Charlotte Bruns-don, in different ways, have analyzed.[21]

The historical spectator, in his/her specificity, is also far more important in the televisual than in the filmic situation, which adds to the need to bring him/her into the apparatus. He/she is crucial to the mechanism because of the sponsors who pay for the programs and whose strategies are ultimately responsible for situating the viewer as endlessly consuming, endlessly in the state of an about-to-be-filled desire.

This state furthers one's televisual sense of existing in some time-less present: neither texts nor the institution of television itself is his-torically situated. MTV in particular blurs distinct separations and boundaries including that between past and present. As will be more clear in Chapter 3, MTV simply takes over the history of rock and roll, flattening out all the distinct types into one continuous present. The teenage audience is now no longer seen as divided into distinct groups addressed by different kinds of rock music but is constituted by the station as one decentered mass that absorbs all the types indiscriminately – without noting or knowing their historical ori-gins.

But this "present" is one that often looks uncannily like a future, postholocaust world, drawing as it does upon imagery from the science fiction film, creating ever greater dislocation of the time dimension. The result is the construction of a decentered, a-historical model spectator that mimics the cultural formation of contemporary teenagers appearing to live in a timeless but implicitly "futurized" present.

But let me now, as Tribe suggests, ask what "the determinate rela-tions" of my own discourse are. First, my discourse is historical in that I am setting up a point of enunciation outside of MTV, from which I examine how its institutional practices construct subjects to the tune of 28 million (as of April 1986). While the relations between MTV as institution and the subjects it constructs do not involve the same kind of power as Foucault's mental, penal, and educational institutions, the station deliberately creates, for its own profit, sub-jects who would not otherwise exist. I am both a subject positioned by MTV as viewer, and a subject using a critical meta-language to distance myself from, and to explain, that positioning.

29

Second, then, as this last point suggests, my discourse emerges from academia; it is situated within an institution whose function is, partly, to produce scholarship. My meta-critical discourse belongs in the academic tradition of cultural studies, and is inevitably shaped by that context.

Third, as a feminist, I bring to MTV a set of reading formations that lead me to resist the gender positions that MTV offers. Other resistances come from the generational gap between myself and the white, middle-American teenager or young adult that MTV addresses (a gap I partially addressed in the Introduction), and who brings to reception far different cultural formations around sex and politics, especially race and class, from mine.

Finally, as this last point implies, we have a situation where the mass of the MTV audience brings to reception reading formations that by and large coincide with those that shape MTV texts. As a commercial form, it is MTV's ability to address current adolescent desires and wish fulfilments, inscribed in an idiom familiar to teenagers, that guarantees its success.

What are some of the cultural codes that structure the majority of MTV programs? How far can we say that these in fact duplicate the reading formations of the station's spectators? To begin with, MTV appears symptomatic of Reagan's America in its unquestioning materialism. Videos for the most part assume an upper-middle-class ambience (note the sleek, modern design settings, the emphasis on luxury items – big cars, fancy clothes, jewelry, contemporary furniture). Only a few videos (and these belong in a special "critical" category, as we'll see) show working-class settings and consciousness.

Another thing that strikes the uninitiated is the frequency of either settings that recall earth prior to civilization or those that suggest a futurist, post-holocaust world. In either case what we have is depersonalization. In the futurist videos, there is an uncritical over-valuing of the machine that is arguably a product of the nuclear age in which teenagers live. (This tendency is evident in the many popular science fiction movies geared to the teenage market. Significantly, the feature of the simulacrum, most common in these movies – viz. *The Man Who Fell to Earth, Blade Runner, Brother From Another Planet* – is not often evident in MTV tapes, presumably because, for commercial reasons, the focus has to be on the live body of the star. But the kind of drugged out, alienated, androgynous doubling found in a film like *Liquid Sky* is present in MTV videos.)

Further, in terms of reading formations, there is the new openness toward sexuality that has been part of this generation's cultural experience. The 1970s and 1980s have witnessed the irruption into consciousness (and often into the daily experiences) of young adults of all varieties of sexuality – bi-sexual, homosexual, sado-masochistic, transvestite, etc. This has evolved partly through the emphasis of the 1970s Women's Movement on sex-roles and female homosexuality and partly through the increasing male gay rights movements and general loosening up of rigid male/female sex-roles, providing a variety of positions for both genders not possible before. Finally, there is the racist aspect of MTV discussed in the Introduction and that reflects aspects of Reagan's America. The largely white, middle-American audience to which MTV gears itself are uninterested in black bands, and this we must attribute to cultural codes that shape this group in Reagan's America.

Nevertheless, as I hope to show later on, MTV's peculiar form means that management cannot contain all the positions shown: the short four-minute texts embedded within a continuous 24-hour flow, leave gaps for some alternate positions. In recent months, following the inspiration of the USA for Africa and Bob Geldof's Live Aid events, there has been a significant increase in videos with working-class settings and social commentary. The Farm Aid and anti-apartheid rock events of Fall 1985, the powerful "Sun-City" video, Cougar-Mellencamp's farm-related "Rainbow Man" video, and feminist videos like Pat Benatar's "Sex As a Weapon" and the Annie Lennox/Aretha Franklin "Sisters Are Doin' It For Themselves," suggest a continuing social concern on the part of rock musicians of all types. However, as we'll see, the placement of the videos within the 24-hour televisual flow often eliminates any possible effectiveness; and there is the further issue of a new kind of "radical chique" around the large fund-raising events that mitigates their oppositional aspects.

As will become evident, beneath this set of sociological "reading formations" lies the address to adolescent desire already noted, which involves the level of the unconscious. Values, narratives,

31

images are organized thematically according to these reading formations, but they are inflected always to satisfy unconscious fantasies,
wish fulfillments, and adolescent ideal-ego formations in the imaginary. This register, in its televisual specificity, will be explored in a
later chapter. Let me note merely that the linking of materialist and
cynical values to the adolescent imaginary repertoire makes teenagers vulnerable to absorption of these values if they do not already
hold them.

   This critique, however, addressed as it is from within the humanist, sociological discourse, may ultimately miss its mark. The categories of the discourse, arguably, are irrelevant to MTV if we view it
as a postmodernist phenomenon. It is here that the specificity of the
televisual apparatus becomes important, since television may itself
be seen as a postmodernist phenomenon in its very construction of a
decentered historical spectator, and its obliteration of hitherto sacrosanct boundaries, such as those between "fiction" and "reality," or
between the space of the viewing-subject and that within the TV
screen. In other words, part of the reading formation for MTV (and
possibly the greater part) is its belonging within a postmodernist discourse that structures not only the psychic and social lives of adoles-
cents but also their dominant entertainment experience, namely
watching TV. It is to this postmodernist discourse as evident in the
aesthetic forms and themes of MTV, as also in the very structuring
of desire in the videos, that I will now turn.

3

MTV and the avant-garde: the emergence of a postmodernist anti-aesthetic?

In this chapter I address the second of the various levels of discourse about MTV and postmodernism, namely that of the ways in which the technical and formal devices of the majority of videos on MTV may be seen to constitute a postmodernist "anti-aesthetic." I will explore first the generally avant-garde techniques of videos on MTV which have led the casual critic to celebrate their subversive aspects. But are the deconstructive, apparently "modernist" devices in fact subversive? How are we to explain them, given MTV's commercial context of production?

Let me briefly survey the techniques that *appear* avant-garde. There is, first, the abandonment of traditional narrational devices of most popular culture hitherto. Cause—effect, time—space, and continuity relationships are often violated, along with the usual conception of "character." Even in videos that seem to retain a loose sort of story, editing devices routinely violate classical Hollywood codes of shot/counter-shot, the 180 degree rule, the 30 degree angle rule, eye-line matches, etc. (See the detailed analysis of Madonna's "Material Girl" in Chapter 5.)

The violation of classical codes is paradoxical in "Material Girl" since the film pastiches Howard Hawkes's *Gentlemen Prefer Blondes*, as will be clear later on. Here "Material Girl" typifies what one first notices about rock videos, namely their frequent reliance on classical Hollywood film genres, whether it be incorporation, parody, pastiche, or ridicule of representations from mainstream cinema that is going on. Many videos early on seemed to take off from standard genres (the most brilliant and complete early example was Michael Jackson's famous video "Thriller," that both used and parodied the gothic/horror genre, as, later, his near-perfect "Billie Jean" did the spy film). Videos like Bonnie Tyler's "Holding Out for a Hero," which relied on the Western; Berlin's "No More Tears," relying on the crime film (specifically *Bonnie and Clyde*); Rockwell's 'Somebody's Watching Me" (depending on the horror film); or, most recently, The Rolling Stones' colorful "Harlem Shuffle" (a cross between Walt Disney and the Broadway musical), stand in a special relationship to the classical cinema and are inconceivable without knowledge of Hollywood. Recently, directors have taken to incorporating certain stars' images in videos (the Romantics' "Talking in Your Sleep" includes images of Marilyn Monroe; Carnes's "Bette Davis' Eyes" takes off from another star), or inserting swift, unmarked clips from Hollywood movies. A recent example of the latter technique is Ratt's "You're in Love," which mocks the whole concept of romantic love as depicted in classical films from Fritz Lang's *Metropolis* to the present, and including clips from Walt Disney, Ingrid Bergman and Peter Lorre movies, and from films with Lucille Ball and Groucho Marx (themselves already in the satiric mode). In between, we have shots of the heavy metal band wearing typical lurid and androgynous outfits in hectic performance in a strobe-lit arena, dramatizing the distance between the largely innocent and romantic Hollywood world and their own contemporary nihilist one. An even more recent example of this use of Hollywood clips is Elton John's "Heartache All Over," which, like the Ratt video, isolates movie love-shots. However, the video takes clips from even further back in the Silent period than did the Ratt one, and here the band are also imaged within a frame, highlighting their awareness of their status as "representations," on the same level as the movie-clips.

Second, videos are routinely, and increasingly, self-reflexive. For instance, we may see the video we are watching being played on a TV monitor within the frame; or the video sets us in the production room in which a rock video is being made that turns out to be the one we are watching (viz. the Rolling Stones's "She Was Hot," Rick

34

MTV AND THE AVANT-GARDE

Springfield's "Someone to Love," Human League's "Don't You Want Me Baby?"). In different ways, two Phil Collins videos, one with Phil Bailey, offer the most extended commentary on video production. The entire narrative of "Easy Lover" (made with Phil Bailey) deals with the tape being made. We are let into the intricacies of the filming, and see the large 35mm camera in the foreground, its video monitor relaying the framing to the camera man; in the rear we see Collins and Bailey rehearsing their act, then being made up, getting properly dressed for the actual filming, taking a lunch break, etc.

Phil Collins's recent "Don't Forget My Number" belongs in a group of videos whose theme is parody of video production as an institution rather than commenting on, and including, the technical processes involved. The thematic parody is carried further than that familiar from Hollywood film commenting on the Hollywood world, but the type is not truly self-reflexive in the manner of videos discussed above. "Don't Forget My Number" begins with Collins's agent leaving him with the pompous director who has been hired to make his new video. The two men compete to see who knows most about popular culture and then try out various ludicrous scenarios for the video, including a mock Western set-up not at all appropriate for Collins. Some of the scenarios tried out parody not only classic film genres but other popular MTV videos, such as the award-winning Cars' "You Might Think," Elton John's videos, or David Lee Roth's successful "California Girls."

David Lee Roth's "Just Like a Gigolo" in a similar vein, begins with a parody of agents, video producers, and directors fawning over an exhausted Roth at the conclusion of what they see as a successful video. Lee Roth however clearly disagrees, and proceeds to imagine the video he would make if left to his own devices. Predictably, the fantasy video is full of surprising events and sexy girls. Steve Perry's "O Sherrie" also begins with a parody of agents, directors, and groupies trying to get the protagonist ready for a video set in the medieval period. Fed up, the hero refuses to comply, and he finally runs off with his girlfriend, leaving behind his exasperated money-and image-conscious entourage.

Dire Straits' "Money For Nothing" comments baldly on MTV itself, and on the alternate blandness and sensationalism of videos shown (as the director, Steve Barron, has noted).[1] The video is already famous for its extraordinarily innovative techniques (Barron had already experimented with "rotoscoping" in the equally famous and creative A-ha video "Take On Me"). Sung by robot figures in the image of working men installing microwave ovens, the video shows them monotonously moving fridges and colour TVs. In the course of their work, they watch rock stars on MTV; as they sing about their tasks, we have images of huge TV screens playing MTV videos and featuring, from time to time, the Dire Straits band. From the robot-workers' point of view, "Playing a guitar on MTV/That ain't working" but "Money for nothing/Chicks for free."

In other videos, the text foregrounds some aspect of the technology involved in video production, again drawing attention to the fact of the text's construction and to the processes of spectatorship. An interesting example is the lively, well-edited, and humorous Mick Jagger/David Bowie "Dancing in the Street" because the first version did *not* include shots of the camera filming the duo. The later one includes a number of such shots, and reveals what the device does; in this case, the effect is to situate the dancing by making the narrative that of filming the dance. Thus the self-reflexivity here paradoxically enhances the "reality-effect" by providing an audience for whom the pair are performing. It is true that the spectator is also made aware of the processes of the text's production, but the two levels become blurred.

In Glen Frey's "The Heat is On" the video is apparently what a man is watching on an editing machine, since the tape begins and ends with the monitor image, while in other videos, like Peter Gabriel's "Shock the Monkey," there is a projector present and running throughout. In this case, the device is disturbing precisely because it is not narratively located or *explained*, as in some of the other cases. A familiar image, direct from Godard and the avant-garde film tradition, is the clap-board being closed in front frame, coming down on the action about to be filmed, and foregrounding production. (A recent example is the start of Tom Petty and the Heartbreakers' "Make It Better.")

Another prevalent deconstructive image is that of a man with a camera taking hidden photographs of a woman (see Eurythmics' "Here Comes the Rain Again" and Rod Stewart's "Infatuation"). A

36

recent Eurythmics' video, "Sexcrime" (in the news because of censorship), imitates Hitchcock's *Vertigo* in the image of a huge close-up of the human eye, inside which we see a camera clicking away. The eye is no longer, as with Vertov, a metaphorical camera but a literal one; the camera-eye has become the camera-I. Even more recently, Duran Duran's "A View to Kill," the video promo for the movie, takes as its entire theme the idea of photography, focusing on the objectification of the female body through the camera lens. Instead of Hitchcock, its dedication is to James Bond (whose logo also seems to imitate *Vertigo*). Voyeurism, always an implicit theme in commercial movies, has recently become an explicit one, especially with a director like Brian De Palma, who is much influenced by Hitchcock. Like *A View to Kill*, his *Body Double* plays with and comments upon the camera's voyeuristic properties, much as do the videos, as I'll show in detail later on.

A new related phenomenon is the representation of the production of the music in the sense of showing the different components and technology of the band that produces the music itself. The video "General Lee" not only pastiches old movies but also shows the band's equipment being assembled. Again, we find an analogue in a contemporary film like the Talking Heads' *Stop Making Sense* (the title itself is significant, as we'll see), which starts with David Byrne standing alone on an empty stage with a cassette recorder, and proceeds to show us the band assembling itself bit by bit with a corresponding increase in and complexity of sound, until it reaches its deafening full strength. David Bowie's "D.J." illustrates the "behind the scenes" aspect of radio, rather than video, while betraying the anarchic, nihilist element of the postmodernist video that I'll discuss later. Bowie's "Blue Jean" comments not only on video production but on the whole rock star phenomenon.

Videos often focus on photographs of the protagonist as a child or in the present, or set up the image in a series of photograph-like frames. Def Leppard's "The Photograph," as its name implies is a classic of the type, but the device is used in many other videos, such as John Cougar's "Jack and Diane" and his successful "Small Town," or Real Life's "Send Me An Angel," where the video is set up as a series of slides being projected onto a screen.

All kinds of framing within the frame are now common; one video sets up a proscenium arch type of frame, with perspective, the image played out on all sides of what is essentially a box. Dateline News, Channel 4, recently picked up the device for its evening news spots, and Aretha Franklin and Annie Lennox's "Sisters Are Doin' It For Themselves" ends with such a box on which are displayed various images from the video. Videos increasingly use a large screen within the screen, set up above or behind the performers' heads and on which we see not only the greatly enlarged images of the players, but also the narrative involved, confusing and destabilizing the spectator/screen relationship. Duran Duran's "Reflex" explicitly plays upon disrupting the spectator/screen relationship when, after seeing the figures of the performers on the huge screen behind their heads, a wave fills the screen and then spills over onto the fans watching the performance.

A variation of these devices may be found in a Bryan Adams video where the performer stands on stage facing the audience of TV sets and has behind him another series of sets containing his own image. Or the video mise-en-scène can consist entirely of TV sets piled up on one another, on which the performer's image is displayed in varying ways as in Asia's "Only Time Will Tell," or Outfield's "All the Love in the World." Daryl Hall and Oats use all kinds of inventive visual devices in their "Out of Touch," including play with a huge screen on which we see the performers imaged while at the same time they are present in front of it. Motels' "Shame On You" has a dialogue between a bored woman trapped in a traditional relationship and a woman on a large ad board outside her window, who suddenly comes alive in various guises in response to the woman's distress. Don Henley's "Boys of Summer" opens with the forlorn hero apparently calling up a movie of his former happiness with his lover. This movie plays behind his head, but then the viewer is taken up into it as it becomes the narrative, only to be later repositioned as a spectator of the movie within the fictional world.

The sanctity of the image of illusionist texts is completely questioned by these devices. But in another set of videos specific violation is done to the image, so that no representation is stable or solid for very long. One of the early videos to play with the image was Yes's "Leave It" (famous for its many versions): here the image was

The Cars, "You might think"

This shot exemplifies the common destruction of illusionism: the band first enter the round photograph of the heroine's dressing table, where they are seen playing; the hero then takes his place beside the heroine in the square photograph, having first removed her old lover.

This image shows the common play with old Hollywood films: here the hero mimics King Kong, in the old movie, hanging onto the Empire State Building with one hand while cradling the heroine, now miniscule, in the other.

39

turned around as a flat, two-dimensional surface and then swept off into space. In Cyndi Lauper's "Girls Just Wanna Have Fun," the image is scrunched up into balls, each with a girl's image on it, that then circle around in space, splitting into many pieces in the process. But perhaps the most outrageous and daring play with the illusionist image is the Cars' now classic video, "You Might Think," in which all manner of surprising and unexpected operations are performed with the image, very much in the style of the French Surrealist painter and sculptor, René Magritte. (This video won the first MTV Academy Award in Fall 1984, presumably for its ingenuity.)

In Emile Benveniste's terms (discussed in Chapter 2), many MTV videos are "discourse" rather than "history" in that they foreground their sources of enunciation and comment on their processes of production. Yet these devices do not go along with an ideologically subversive stance toward dominant culture as in the "proper" avant-garde text of Benveniste's model. The aesthetic discourse dominant in western culture from the late nineteenth to the mid-twentieth century has polarized the popular/realist commercial text and the "high art" modernist one, making impossible a text that was at once avant-garde and popular. And yet this is what MTV apparently is.

The discourse of contemporary film theory has continued the distinctions basic to dominant aesthetic discourse, if for different reasons. The classical Hollywood text has been conceived as producing the "reality effect" specifically through effacement of the means of production. That is why both Metz and Geoffrey Nowell-Smith, as we saw earlier, categorized the classical text as "history" – the "story told from nowhere, told by nobody but received by someone, without whom it would not exist." Devices like shot/counter-shot, continuity editing, the 180 degree rule and so on, give the spectator the illusion of creating the images, suturing him/her into the narrative flow. Theorists have claimed that it is the very "reality-effect" produced through these devices that ensures the texts remaining safely within dominant ideological constructs. Avant-garde texts, on the other hand, have been seen as able to embody ideology subversive of bourgeois hegemony because their aesthetic strategies are set up in deliberate opposition to classical realist forms. The self-reflexivity of modernist texts together with the self-conscious play with dominant

Table 1   Polarized filmic categories in recent film theory

The classical text (Hollywood)	The avant-garde text
Realism/narrative	Non-realist anti-narrative
History	Discourse
Complicit ideology	Rupture of dominant ideology

forms often included (at least in the *political* modernist text) a critique of mainstream culture (see Table 1).

The above polarized categories obviously do not fit MTV, and it is this very blurring of hitherto sacrosanct conceptual boundaries and polarities, in terms of both aesthetic forms and critical categories, that marks the station as a postmodernist form. The short, four-minute span, the origin of the form in advertising and the song-image format (which defies many Hollywood conventions) as we already saw seems to require different critical conceptions. But if we add in the prevalence of deconstructive devices, we clearly need new theoretical formulations to explain what is going on.

The main differences between MTV and the classical Hollywood film arise from the structuring of the station as a 24-hour continuous flow with its three- to four-minute texts (often non-narrative or non-Oedipal narrative), and from the song-image format. First, a word about the structure that offers a decentered position for the spectator, far different from the sutured, Hollywood film spectator mentioned above: on the one hand, there are the constant interruptions caused by the ending of one video and the start of the next, by the veejay's comments, introductions, interviews, and by the ads; on the other, there is the absence of the cause—effect narrative of the Freudian "family romance" type that film theorists have described. Together, these elements prevent the kind of regression to Oedipal primary processes possible in the cinema through the prolonged narrative identification, and through the devices of shot/counter-shot, etc., mentioned earlier. The whole construction of the cinematic apparatus, with the projection in a darkened room and the voyeuristic play of the lit screen with larger than life figures upon it, encourages in the cinema regression to Oedipal childhood processes (particularly the voyeuristic/fetishistic gaze) much discussed by film theorists.

The cinema has also been theorized as re-evoking the Lacanian mirror phase, particularly for the male spectator. Because Lacan's theories of the way the subject is constructed in a patriarchal language order have been so influential in recent film theory, and since the model clearly needs adapting to the television context, let me briefly outline aspects of his theory that will be central to my discussion here and elsewhere in the book. It is Lacan's distinction between the imaginary and the symbolic, in which woman is relegated to the position of absence, or lack, that has preoccupied film theorists.

For Lacan, the imaginary *proper* lacks specificity – or rather, it brings both genders into the feminine through the illusory sense of being merged with the mother. What Lacan calls the "mirror-phase" (the moment when the child first sets up a relationship to its image in the mirror) marks the awareness of the illusoriness of oneness with the mother. The child, that is, begins to be aware of the mother as an object distinct from itself (the mirror contains an image of the mother holding the child); it also recognizes its "mirror" self (which Lacan calls an ideal imago) as an entity distinct from itself.[2] The subject is thus constituted as a *split* subject (i.e. both mother and non-mother; this side of the mirror and within the mirror). It is important that the ideal ego constructed during this mirror-phase is not entirely on the side of the imaginary in that the child introjects the image of the mother as *another image*; it begins to symbolize thus its own look as that of the Other, and to set in motion the desire for the mother (displaced as we'll see into a desire for what she desires) that will persist through its life.

This symbolization of the mother as the Other is for Lacan a universal experience and one that is essential for the human-to-be to in fact become *human*. The individuation that the level of symbolizing involves is a necessary development; the mother–child dyad must be interrupted by the language order if the child is not to remain down in the level of the imaginary. The mirror-phase thus prepares the child for its subsequent entry into the realm of the symbolic (by which Lacan means the language and other signifying and representational systems, such as images, gestures, sound, etc.), in which

42

the child takes up its position as a "sexed" being (it recognizes various subject positions such as "he," "she," "you," "it").[3] Because signifying systems are organized around the phallus as the prime signifier, for Lacan the woman occupies the place of lack or absence. The boy and girl child thus find themselves in vastly different positions vis-à-vis the dominant order once they enter the realm of the symbolic.

The problem for the girl is in being positioned so as to identify with the mother, which means desiring what the mother desires, namely the phallus. This desire has nothing to do with anything essential or biological about the girl but everything to do with the way that the symbolic is organized. Lacan's system, in fact, frees us from the tyranny of the biological.[4]

Roland Barthes has, perhaps better than anyone, described the nature of the "lure" of the film image that he equates with the "lure" of the infant's mirror image:

> The image is there before me, for my benefit: coalescent (signifier and signified perfectly blended), analogical, global, pregnant; it is a perfect lure. I pounce upon it as an animal snatches up a "life-like" rag. Of course, the image maintains (in the subject that I think I am) a miscognition attached to the ego and to the imaginary. In the movie theater . . . I glue nose, to the point of disjointing it, on the mirror of the screen, to the imaginary other with which I identify myself narcissistically.[5]

Barthes shows how the cinematic viewer tries to recover the original illusory plenitude that precedes the mirror phase, and that is temporarily duplicated during the mirror phase in the misrecognition of the infant's image as him/herself, but more perfect. But the televisual apparatus, as described earlier, is not the kind to produce this sort of effect. This means that the MTV text cannot be viewed in the same way as the dream text that the film spectator imagines she/he is producing. Nor, as we'll see, can we talk of MTV being geared to the same kind of male voyeuristic/fetishistic gaze that film largely relies on. (The whole issue of gender address will be discussed in Chapter 5.) In terms of the Lacanian paradigm outlined above, MTV, like most television, rather positions the subject at the moment of discovery of split subjectivity that follows the stage of illusory miscognition of unity with the ideal image. The aesthetic devices of many videos evoke not plenitude but precisely split subjectivity (the images in all those TV screens or movie screens within TV screens); but the very evocation of split subjectivity calls up the desire for plenitude which we somehow hope to achieve by continued consumption which keeps us at least from lapsing into emptiness.

Or does it? Are "fullness" or "emptiness" still relevant terms? Baudrillard, for instance, has argued that the televisual apparatus manifests a new stage of consciousness, which he calls the "universe of communication," in which all we have are "simulations," there being no "real" external to them. This means that we have a universe in which "fiction" and "reality" coalesce in a realm of "simulacra." The universe replaces the old one in which people *believed* that "fiction" copied some original that was "real."[6] The new postmodern universe, with its celebration of the look – the surfaces, textures, the self-as-commodity – threatens to reduce everything to the image/representation/simulacrum. Television, with its decentered address, its flattening out of things into a network or system, the parts of which all rely on each other, and which is endless, unbounded, unframed, seems to embody the new universe; and within television, MTV in particular manifests the phenomena outlined by Baudrillard.

Perhaps most relevant to our discussion of the postmodernist devices in MTV videos generally is the blurring of distinctions between a "subject" and an "image." What seems to be happening in the play with the image of the various kinds discussed is the reduction of the old notion of "self" to an "image" merely. Television in this way seems to be at the end of a whole series of changes begun at the turn of the century with the development of modern forms of advertising and of the department-store window.[7] A second major change was the invention of the cinematic apparatus, and television has produced the last round of changes; its screen now replaces the cinema screen as the controlling cultural mode, setting up a new spectator—screen relationship that is evident in the plethora of devices described above. This will I think be more clear in the detailed analyses in the next chapters.

To the degree that MTV is still a narrative form, we have a new *kind* of story that reflects this changed relationship of image to self.

It makes little sense to talk about the self-reflexive devices of MTV defying dominant ideology through a deliberate undercutting of illusionism, since that discourse and its language I have argued is irrelevant to the new MTV phenomenon. MTV videos embody a new story about what the machine can do, and within that story it abandons traditional illusionism by blurring the "fiction/reality" distinction.

Modernism is itself partly responsible for this: its strategies have become assimilated into the dominant culture, so that the spectator cannot be shocked any more in the old ways. The representation of a representation is no longer inherently subversive as in modernism. And it is in the very effacement of previously distinct boundaries and separations, particularly those between high and popular forms that we have been discussing, that MTV reveals itself, arguably, as a postmodernist form.

In a well-known essay, "Postmodernism and consumer society,"[8] Fredric Jameson has defined postmodernism negatively. He is concerned about the "disappearance of the sense of history" and the living in a perpetual present which, following Lacan and Baudrillard, he associates with the schizophrenic state. For Lacan, as for Jameson, schizophrenia is an effect of language, the refusal to enter the realm of the symbolic. Instead of signifiers and signified in postmodernist texts being coherently organized in a comprehensive chain, the flow of words or images is such that the reader/spectator cannot associate any meaning or recognize boundaries and differences, past and present. She/he rather is coaxed into what Jameson calls the postmodernist, schizophrenic stance – that of being fixated on the detached signifier, isolated in a present from which there is no escape.

This return to an eternal, undifferentiated present is an attempt to return to the realm of the imaginary in which there was no self and Other, merely an illusory, timeless continuum. Louis Sass has provocatively tried to link clinically defined schizophrenic states with modernism;[9] while this is interesting, I think it more correct to see the schizophrenic stance as a *postmodernist* phenomenon. For modernism, as Jameson points out, still retains a position from which it speaks. It attempts to critique bourgeois culture through the creation of a unique style that was "subversive and embattled" in its time. Jameson cites "Abstract Expressionism, the great

45

modernist poetry of Pound, Eliot or Wallace Stevens; the International Style (Le Corbusier, Frank Lloyd Wright, Mies); Stravinsky; Joyce, Proust, Mann . . . '' (p. 111). Thought to be "scandalous or shocking to our grandparents," these are now, "for the generation which arrives at the gate in the '60s – felt to be the establishment and the enemy – dead, stifling, canonical, the reified monuments one has to destroy to do anything new" (p. 112).

Postmodernism is partly defined by its reaction to earlier modernist models, but it uses pastiche in the place of the modernist parody. Modernism often parodied the increasingly industrialist and consumerist society in an attempt to position it critically; but postmodernism, according to Jameson, is precisely fascinated by what modernism tried to take a stance against, namely "the whole landscape of advertising and motels, of the Las Vegas strip, of the late show and the Grade-B Hollywood film, of so-called paraliterature with its airport paperback categories of gothic and romance, the popular biography, the murder mystery and the science fiction or fantasy novel" (p. 112). While modernism often parodied such things, postmodernism merely uses pastiche, a "neutral practice of mimicry . . . without that still latent feeling that there exists something *normal* compared to which what is being imitated is rather comic" (p. 114).

If one accepts Jameson's argument, then MTV's preference for pastiche reveals its lack of orienting boundaries; in this case, like much postmodernist art in Jameson's view, rock videos incorporate, rather than quote, other texts, "to the point where the link between high art and commercial forms seems increasingly difficult to draw." MTV refuses any clear recognition of previously sacred aesthetic boundaries: images from German Expressionism, French Surrealism, and Dadism (Fritz Lang, Bunuel, Magritte, and Dali) are mixed together with those pillaged from the noir, gangster, and horror films in such a way as to obliterate differences (see The Cars' "You Might Think"). Indeed, the constant reference to Hollywood film genres, particularly the western, film noir, the detective film, the science fiction film, is pervasive, as noted earlier (i.e. Bonnie Tyler's "Holding Out for a Hero," and Devo's "Whip It" (the western); Mama's Boys' "Mama, We're All Crazy Now" (Hitchcock); Sting's "Fortress Around Your Heart" (detective); Sammy Hagar's "V.O.A." (spy film)).

For Jameson, such eliding of forms indicates the end of any critical cultural position, a dangerous lack of the ability to speak from a particular place and to make distinctions. While there is some justification for this kind of concern, it seems to miss possible positive aspects of the effacement of hitherto sacred boundaries. Jameson's Marxist critique retains the notion of history as a discourse that speaks from a perspective of "truth," and this, as we've seen, is problematic. It may prevent Jameson from seeing how the very defiance of a historical positioning may be progressive. In the case of MTV, video artists are often playing with standard high art and popular culture images in a self-conscious manner, creating a liberating sense by the very defiance of traditional boundaries. Images from both high and low art are now arguably clichéd, threadbare, archaic in the computer and space age. Rock videos may be seen as revitalizing the dead images by juxtaposing and re-working them in new combinations that avoid the old polarities. This may be the only strategy available to young artists struggling to find their place in society and to create new images to represent the changed situation they find themselves in.

MTV's construction of a decentered spectator indicates recognition of the alienated world teenagers confront. Nevertheless, individual videos themselves often construct a brief "centered" effect, intended to mediate the overall possibly unpleasurable decentering and to keep the spectator watching. The overall commercial framework of MTV (as of all television) requires, as we've seen, locking the spectator into the hypnotized state of *impending* satisfaction; "centering" must take place for short periods if the requisite consumption mechanism is to work. In the case of MTV, the "centering" effect is produced by the song-image format and the constant return to the lip-synching face of the rock star who is being "sold" in any particular video.

This particular song-image format represents one of the main differences between the rock video and the classical Hollywood film. Not even the Hollywood musical is useful here as a model. I will deal with this issue in detailed analyses of particular videos in the next chapters, so let me merely note here that in the rock video, we find images evoked by song words (obviously arbitrary, quixotic even), and relayed through the voice and face of the rock star and band members. Most often, as already noted, there is no narrative proper (there may be loosely linked narrative suggestions), and nothing corresponding to the Hollywood conception of "character." It is the return to the human face that prevents the disconnected image-series from becoming unpleasurable in the manner of the truly avant-garde text. The dominant construction in videos replaces the Hollywood suturing of the spectator in the images through shot/counter-shot with a constant return to the centering close-up of the lip-synching face of the singer. This, together with the musical rhythm/tones/sounds and the rock star's voice, holds together otherwise disparate images and incoherent signifieds.

But the "gaze" involved in the brief "centering" moments is far from the monolithic one of the classical Hollywood film, largely because the televisual apparatus, with its arrangement of a series of short, constantly changing segments (in place of the two-hour continuous film narrative) enables the production of a variety of gazes. In the next chapter, I will outline the main kinds of "gaze" that occur within the 24-hour MTV televisual flow in the video segments, but will leave full discussion of gender address in the gaze until Chapter 5. There, bearing in mind Baudrillard's theory of the televisual apparatus, we will see the new kinds of narrative as they deviate from the old, classical Oedipal ones. Chapter 4 will focus mainly on themes in the socially conscious video.

4

Ideology, adolescent desire, and the five types of video on MTV

If Lacan did not actually use the term the "social imaginary," this is implied by his general discussion of the imaginary/symbolic polarity in the sense that every child apparently moves through the *same* imaginary and enters the *same* symbolic (i.e. the langauge and other representational orders). But both the imaginary and the symbolic are social in a more specific sense – a sense that involves particular historical and cultural context. The cultural/historical embeddedness of the symbolic is obvious in the post-structuralist era, but less obvious may be the social nature of that imaginary that continues alongside the symbolic, enmeshed with it in the manner of secondary with primary processes, and which harnesses the insatiable desire instituted at the moment of individuation. While the infant's early, pre-symbolic psychic experience (the mother–child dyad) may vary rather little from one culture or historical period to another, the post-symbolic imaginary is surely inflected by cultural and historical specificities.

What I am calling the post-symbolic imaginary combines Lacan's notions of the subject split at the moment of entry into the symbolic with Althusser's conception of Ideological State Apparatuses. It is the splitting of the subject into an entity both mother and not-mother; this side of the mirror and within the mirror that sets up the structure of the ideal imago that will remain after entry into the symbolic. The subject, that is, will forever yearn, unconsciously, for the

49

illusory state of plenitude that it experienced before the mirror phase. The symbolization of its own look as that of the Other that takes place in the mirror phase makes the subject vulnerable to subjection to a transcendental Subject which Lacan identifies as the phallus, Althusser more generally as "ideology." According to Althusser, this ideology interpellates individuals as subjects: all ideology, he says, is "specular, i.e. a mirror-structure, and *doubly* specular: this mirror duplication is constitutive of ideology and ensures its functioning."[1] In ideology, the absolute Subject occupies the centre, interpellating individuals around it into subjects "in a double mirror-connexion such that it *subjects* the subjects to the Subject, while giving them in the Subject, in which each subject can contemplate its own image (present and future), the guarantee that this really concerns them and Him" (p. 180). For Althusser, that is, ideology turns individuals into subjects by "hailing" them, and is thus a necessary part of human social organization.

But the specific form of that ideology will vary from culture to culture and from one historical period to another since, for Althusser, "Ideology is a 'representation' of the imaginary relationship of individuals to their real conditions of existence" (p. 162). The specific *kinds* of ideal imagos that predominate in any concrete cultural context will obviously vary and they will change as, on a level of which the individual is not aware, his/her "real" conditions of existence change.

One of the Ideological State Apparatuses that Althusser mentions but does not examine is television. Writing in 1969, Althusser was not yet aware of television's specific cultural impact, of its role in developing what Baudrillard has called the new, "cold" universe of communication with its profound changes in the relationship of subject to image suggested in the last chapter. We saw that while the movie screen harnesses the subject's desire in terms of subjection to a transcendental Subject, appearing momentarily to provide the longed-for plenitude, the TV screen rather keeps the subject in the position of discovery of split subjectivity before the mirror and of the actual ensuing *decenteredness*. The TV screen's constantly changing "texts," of whatever kind, provide the constant *promise* of a plenitude forever deferred.

Baudrillard takes things a step further, arguing that the TV screen symbolizes a new era in which "The Faustian, Promethean (perhaps Oedipal) period of production and consumption" has given way to "the narcissistic and protean era of connections, contact, contiguity, feedback and generalized interface that goes with the universe of communication."[2] By this, Baudrillard means that the whole earlier "intimate" universe (in his words, "projective, imaginary and symbolic" (p. 126)), with its domestic scene, interiority, private space-time correlative to a public space – all this is disappearing. "Instead," he says, "there is a screen and a network. In place of the reflexive transcendence of mirror and scene, there is the nonreflecting surface, an immanent surface where operations unfold – the smooth operational surface of communication" (pp. 126-7). He concludes that "with the television image – the television being the ultimate and perfect object for this era – our own body and the whole surrounding universe become a control screen."

For Baudrillard, this entails a dramatically different relationship of the subject to objects: for him, people no longer project themselves into their objects in the old ways of getting psychological gratification out of them. If the psychological dimension can still be marked out, "one feels that it is not really there that things are being played out" (p. 127). We have instead a "tactic of potentialities linked to usage." Baudrillard is here talking about the automobile, but what he says applies equally to the television set, to which we likewise relate in terms of "mastery, control and command, an optimalization of the play of possibilities" rather than as "an object of psychological sanctuary" (p. 127). (See Table 2.)

I quote at such length because Baudrillard's predictions are

Table 2 Chart summarizing Baudrillard's and Callois's scheme

Old *"hot"* universe		New *"cold"* universe	
Investment ⎫ Desire ⎬ Expression Passion ⎬ Competition Seduction ⎭		Hazard ⎧ Ecstasy Chance ⎨ Obscenity Vertigo ⎬ Fascination ⎩ Communication	
Processes of hysteria (female) and paranoia (male)		Processes of schizophrenia, elimination of boundaries, exteriorization of the interior	

significant enough to warrant examination in relation to MTV, the channel par excellence where the phenomena he outlines would be taking place. How true is it that "we no longer live in the drama of alienation" (Marx's world) but rather in that of "the ecstasy of communication" (p. 130)? How true is it that the old "hot, sexual obscenity" (the world of Freud) has been succeeded by "the cold and communicational, contractual and motivational obscenity of today" (p.131)?[3]

This has important implications for understanding the issue of "ideology" in MTV: given its roots in blues and jazz, it is not surprising that rock music has traditionally (and especially since the 1960s) embodied a liberal or left humanist position. If the televisual apparatus manifests a new stage of consciousness in which that liberal/left humanism no longer has a place, this implicates the roots of rock.

The social imaginary that I will explore in MTV (in this and the next chapter) has been constructed through the contradictory post-1960s historical moment in which rock videos arise as a mass popular culture form. It is the mapping in the 1980s of the new 1960s discourses about politics, sex, and romance onto the increasingly high-tech stage of an already advanced capitalism that produces the extraordinary MTV imaginary. MTV partly exploits the imaginary desires allowed free play through the various liberation movements, divesting them, for commercial reasons, of their originally revolutionary implications, reducing them largely to the "radical chic" and the pornographic; but its chosen non-stop, 24-hour format of short, four-minute texts inevitably enables expression of positions critical of the status quo not necessarily favored by the institution. But, given Baudrillard's conceptualizations above, we need to analyze how far these "alternate" positions in fact have anything behind them – any on-going alternate politics in the realm of the social formation. How far do the left/humanist positions have referents? How far are they, like much else on MTV, mere simulacra, with nothing *behind*, mere representations, images?[4]

Obviously, the specifically commercial nature of MTV is relevant to this question: the main aim of the channel is consumption, as we've seen, and it thus follows that the overall address cannot be on the level of ideas or values per se, but of what "look" will *sell*. The level of any one text's production – in which individuals might

52

have artistic ambitions and an aesthetic (or even an anti-aesthetic) end in mind – is completely irrelevant once a video is accepted by MTV. For then, the video becomes a commodity to be circulated in a particular fashion by the channel's personnel. It is completely out of the hands of the original producers and of the performers as well.

In MTV, then, we have an altogether different and more encompassing level of commercialization of rock than hitherto. Earlier promoters at least manipulated live bodies, who could resist in certain ways; but now the "materials" that are manipulated, positioned, circulated in a certain fashion are *simulations* which begin to *replace* the "real." The situation is further complicated by the subversive roots that historically shaped rock and roll and that in the 1960s had "referents" in the social formation. Are these radical traces evident on MTV? What is MTV's relationship to the history of rock and roll?

The 24-hour flow is partly responsible for effacing the original address to specific, delimited youth rock audiences. MTV gathers up into itself the history of rock and roll, rendering the originally distinct subject positions merely nostalgic reflection on earlier periods. (This is most clear in the nostalgic return to 1950s styles and sounds, epitomized in the Ramones' "Rock and Roll High School" video.) The relationship of MTV as text to the historical discourse of rock and roll constructed by critics such as Jahn and Cohn, or more recently by Lawrence Grossberg, is interesting in terms of the uses it makes of that discourse in *its* discourses. The three recent phases of rock and roll that critics have identified—1960s soft-rock, 1970s punk and acid rock (often critical of the establishment), and 1980s heavy metal, and new wave rock (nihilist, anarchic) have each been seen historically as addressing distinct teenage communities, distinguished by dress and stance toward the establishment. MTV takes over this discourse, reproducing all of the three main types (there are of course many sub-types that do not appear on MTV, such as reggae or funk), but popularizing and trivializing them into a common "pop" dimension; and then flattening them out into one continuous present of the 24-hour flow, eliding the basic historical addresses. Even the old 1960s and 1970s groups who are still featured (e.g. the Stones, Supertramp) or band members from those decades now going out on their own (e.g. Phil Collins of Genesis,

John Fogerty of Credence Clearwater, Joe Walsh of the Eagles, Pete Townshend of the Who, Eric Clapton, or lesser known returning stars, like Huey Lewis) are simply inserted along with all the rest, without any positioning. In similar fashion, the teenage audience is now no longer seen as divided into distinct groups addressed by the different kinds of rock, but is one decentered mass that absorbs all the types without noting (or knowing) their historical origins, for these have been all but erased, traces remaining only in some aspects of dress and, occasionally, in relation to 1950s mock revivals, in black and white photography.

The erasing of the specific historical address inevitably involves a corollary diminution of specific political or ideological comment. Videos do not even manifest the phenomenon of youth culture searching for a position from which to speak, or concluding that there is no position from which to speak. We rather have the displacement of what we earlier *called* ideology into the new era of the "look," "style," "self-as-commodity," all of which suggest postmodernism. In any case, the effort of MTV managers to bring rock into mainstream culture entails a dilution of originally oppositional stances, or even, as we've seen, censoring of groups, like punk or black bands, that stand too far toward the edges of dominant culture. (If one looks only at MTV one might conclude that rock is dead, or that it has come to the end of its line. In fact, innovative and important music is being developed outside of this "mainstreaming," but is only heard or seen by those aficionados who make efforts to follow developments.)

In exploring further the issue of what specific *kinds* of ideologies we find on MTV, or indeed of whether or not the word "ideology" has any meaning in a postmodern universe, at least of the Baudrillardean variety, I want to distinguish five different types of video that dominate the 24-hour MTV flow. As always, the point in establishing any categories is first to make manageable what is, at least in this case, a huge and unmanageable mass of material, and second to establish a few broadly defined types which are archetypal rather than anything else. That is, rather few videos may actually fit precisely the specific types; but those types offer a schema to which nearly all the videos can be related. They *approximate* rather than *embody* the types. (See Table 3.)

54

Table 3 Five main types of video on MTV

		Romantic	Socially conscious	Nihilist	Classical	Post-modernist
				Modes (all use avant-garde strategies, especially self-reflexivity, play with the image, etc.)		
Predominant MTV themes	Style	Narrative	Elements varied	Performance Anti-narrative	Narrative	Pastiche No linear images
	Love/Sex	Loss and reunion (Pre-Oedipal)	Struggle for autonomy Love as problematic	Sadism/masochism Homoeroticism Androgyny (Phallic)	The male gaze (Voyeuristic fetishistic)	Play with Oedipal positions
	Authority	Parent figures (positive)	Parent and public figures Cultural critique	Nihilism Anarchy Violence	Male as subject Female as object	Neither for nor against authority (ambiguity)

I also want to historicize my own development of this schema: when I began this study in 1982, MTV was far less "postmodern" than it now is. The "socially conscious" video, for instance, was prevalent and had still "behind" it a kind of 1960s politics. Some of the videos I will now put under that heading raise all the issues of the new "radical chic" and of the Baudrillardean "simulacrum" mentioned above. There have been corresponding changes in the romantic video, which I will explain, and in addition changes in the frequency and regularity of cycling of various types over the years. The postmodern video, for instance, seems to extend further and further into the channel in 1986, threatening to take over as the dominant kind.

There are five basic types of video on MTV, three of which seemed, when I first developed the scheme, to correspond roughly to the three types of rock music that have been developed over the past twenty years as noted above (p. 5). I have thus labeled three types "romantic" (i.e. looking back to 1960s soft rock, popularized); "socially conscious" or "modernist" (deriving vaguely from rock groups in the 1960s and 1970s that took oppositional stances); and "nihilist" (deriving from heavy metal, here watered down). That is, in 1982 I felt that these videos still had some special kind of relationship to the (then) recent history of rock music. As we move further away from the 1960s and as the postmodern universe seems increasingly here, so these types begin to reflect merely a different "look" rather than specifically to embody what we may loosely call different "ideologies."

The fourth kind I call "classical" because it adheres more than the others to narrative codes (not necessarily following Hollywood strictly), often being set in realistic environments and eschewing the usual play on the figures of the performing band members. Once again, this type also seems increasingly self-conscious about what it is doing so as to fall into a postmodern "pastiche." In other words, all of what earlier seemed to reflect distinct modes of address now seem ultimately to fall under the "postmodern," which is a term that I had earlier reserved for a specific type of video that even then refused to position itself vis-à-vis what it showed. I still keep the postmodernist video as a separate type, embodying in an extreme form what many videos now evidence.

56

THE FIVE TYPES OF VIDEO

The terms along the top of Table 3 distinguish videos in relation to their overall style and tone: music, words, visuals all create a mood that categorizes the video. Underneath the word "mode" are listed the various techniques that characterize all videos, such as avant-garde devices (self-reflexivity, play with the image), pastiche, the foregrounding of performance, the use of choreographed dance that links some videos with the Hollywood musical. While any of these devices may be found across the three modes, generally the romantic and classical videos use a degree of narrative and less focus on musical instruments and the band in performance (their gender address differs markedly however); the postmodernist videos, at the other extreme, use more pastiche, less self-reflexivity and are characterized mainly by their refusal to take a position toward what they show; their positioning in the realm of *simulacra,* with no gestures toward a signified, sets them apart from other videos.

In between, there is the nihilist video, usually featuring heavy metal bands and often giving most screen time to images of the performers on stage (live concert footage is spliced together, sometimes with other interspersed shots away from the stage); and the "socially conscious" type, defined more by its surface themes than specific visual devices.

Along the side of Table 3 are the themes that dominate all the videos, but the words in the box indicate the differing treatment of the themes in each video type. As will be clear, discussion of "themes" assumes a text's involvement in a signified, and what I have been suggesting is that there is less and less assumption being made about that signified. Thus we have to take the word "theme" as a mere counter for discussing videos that continue to construct stories in which events take place. The same applies to psychological dilemmas portrayed, and for which I have used Freudian terminology in the table; i.e. we must also take these terms as "counters" rather than as having literal application. As Baudrillard noted, despite the psychological level being there, things often seem to be played out *somewhere else.*

Implicit in the table is that MTV, arguably like television as a whole, includes a wide range of gazes with different gender implications in contrast to the (largely) monolithic gaze of the Hollywood film. The televisual apparatus is not gender specific in its modes of functioning, as arguably the filmic apparatus is. Across the various ad-segments we find a variety of "gazes" that indicate an address to a certain kind of male or female imaginary. I will argue that there is frequently a genderless address, and that people of both genders are able to undertake multiple identifications, although this will vary from video type to video type.

As a preliminary, let me say something brief about each kind of video and then proceed in this chapter to analyze the ideological "imaginary" in select videos. I will look here at political meanings in some "socially conscious" videos and then in Chapter 5 study the markedly different kinds of "erotic" imaginary in videos figuring male and female stars. As should be obvious, I am not imputing any authorial control to the historical star subjects being discussed here, since how much control a star has in any one case is unclear; my focus is on *texts* rather than stars. Videos produced for stars in no way attempt to construct an image constant from one text to another; a star's image will depend on what seems most marketable at the particular moment, and on the general style/tone/image of the single, or the record from which the single comes. Since selling the record is the base-line, that will control the "look" of the video being made for sale of the song and its record.

The romantic type, as noted, looks back to the 1960s soft rock, now popularized and sentimentalized. A year or so ago, this type was largely the province of female stars, like the Cyndi Lauper of that time, and tended to address the female spectator. Lionel Ritchie, with his poignant, haunting "Hello," was an exception. The type as a whole was not frequent on the station, nihilist, classical, and alternative types predominating.

In the past years, important changes have taken place: first, in 1983-4 the romantic video increased in number, while the nihilist one declined. Second, male stars took over the romantic type, which routinely headed the MTV Top Twenty Charts (viz. Phil Collins's "One More Night," Foreigner's "I Want to Know What Love is," Paul Young's "Everytime You Go Away"). Currently (mid-1986), the romantic video is generally on the decline, the nihilist and postmodern on the increase, while there are profound changes in both the classical and socially conscious types.

It is the overall nostalgic, sentimental and yearning quality that

58

defines the romantic video. A love relationship, usually male/ female but it can be parent/child or parent-substitute (viz. the 1983 videos, Denise Williams's "Let's Hear It For The Boy," or Lee Carey's "A Fine, Fine Day"), is presented as central to the protagonist's life, something that would "solve" all problems. The address is to the absent or lost loved one, or the video plays out the pain of separation, as in Cyndi Lauper's "Time After Time." Occasionally, the romantic video shows celebration of a love union (as in Pat Benatar's "We Belong," or Stevie Nicks's "If Anyone Falls in Love").

Usually in romantic videos the images are linked in a narrative chain that reproduces the song lines about love, loss, reunion. But it is a weak narrative chain, the main focus being on the emotions of loss or reunion rather than on the causes, conditions or effects of such loss. Cyndi Lauper's "Time After Time" has an unusually complicated narrative, beginning as it does with a typical moment of pastiche as the heroine is inspired to leave her lover by the poignant, bitter-sweet parting on the television screen of Dietrich and Gary Cooper. Before she leaves, the heroine recalls her past with her lover, and we have scenes of his distaste for her wild outfits, of her longing for her working-class mother's comfort, which in turn evoke happy memories of their times together. Catching her in the act of leaving, Lauper's lover takes her to the station, the heroine stopping by to wish her mother farewell before the poignant parting scene at the station. (Lauper's other well-known early video, "Girls Just Want to Have Fun," takes a different stance, and will be discussed under the "socially conscious" type. Most recently, her work falls into the nihilist category, if "Money Changes Everything" is typical of what she will do. Perhaps a bitter comment on her own success, this performance video shows an angry Lauper, shouting out her words and storming around the stage in sneakers, kicking oil drums and twisting and turning in an undirected rage.)

The close, overtly stated mother–daughter bonding in "Time After Time" is significant in foregrounding what I think has increasingly become a sub-text of the romantic video by both male and female stars. Videos in this category idealize parent–child relationships, manifesting pre-Oedipal, bisexual yearnings in the urge to merge with the loved one and recapture infant mother–child closeness. In the early versions of the type, however, close parent—child relationships were usually mother/son (cf. Denise Williams's "Let's Hear It For the Boy") or father/son (cf. Lee Carey's "A Fine, Fine Day," where the close father/son bonding is set off by images of a cold, inadequate mother). Paul Young's video, "Every Time You Go Away," which will be analyzed in detail shortly, arguably exemplifies an interesting genderless address, although the video may be seen as falling into the traditional male yearning for the lost mother object, as we'll see.

As might be expected, the music in these videos is tuneful, melodious, lyrical. Instrumentation is light, often focused on one instrument (like Phil Collins on the piano), and the melodious, main theme is frequently repeated. In the background there is usually a reassuring, steady beat. The star's voice is in the foreground, leading the instruments, and a choir may be pulled in for echo effect. Drums, if used, are soft-pedalled, muffled.

The nihilist video, meanwhile, retains some of the originally anarchic positions of recent punk, new wave and heavy metal bands. On MTV, the type is represented mainly by the heavy metal bands, punk being a sub-group largely censored as too far to the cultural margins. Lawrence Grossberg has focused on the negativity of punk and heavy metal: "It reveals," he notes, "a self-reflexive affirmation of difference, a decathexis of any affirmation."[5] But what impresses me is the paradoxical linking of an overall vitality and creativity (evident in the musical compositions, the visuals, and their combination) with a nihilistic ideology.

Most, but not all, nihilist videos show their origins in live concerts by retaining the performance set-up. The camera focuses on the figures comprising the band, seen playing their instruments in often hectic style on the stage, while we see fans' arms waving in front of the image or else at the rear of an image shot from the performers' point of view. These videos differ from the romantic ones in their aggressive use of camera and editing; wide-angle lenses, zoom shots, rapid montage, typify devices used. In the non-performance type, one image rarely has much to do with the next, and lighting techniques in all of them derive from film noir and German Expressionism. As in those film genres, the world of these videos is unstable, alien. A common image is the sudden, unmotivated explosion, shattering the filmic world and underscoring the violence that lurks beneath (e.g. David Bowie's "D.J."). The stage is often made to look like a strange, deserted landscape simply through lighting devices, or is translated into a disorienting space, as in Ozzy Osbourne's "Shot in the Dark" or Motley Crue's "Home Sweet Home"; but sometimes the performers are seen in non-stage expressionist environments, hanging as it were in outerspace, in a shadowy, undefined, hazy place (as for example in Scorpions' "Rock You Like a Hurricane," analyzed in detail later on, or their recent "No One Like You").

The intensity and concentrated shock effects of these videos produce images that violate those in dominant culture, especially in the area of sexual representation and gender address, which I'll discuss shortly. But the music is equally disorienting and disturbing. Instrumentation is here complex, varied, unmelodious. Drums often roar, while the electric guitars are made to screech and scream and wail. Musical themes often work against each other, and in opposition to the usually screaming voice of the star. The rhythm is driving, relentless, apparently almost out of control at times. Deafening sounds drive out the words, and the performers leap violently about the stage, often bashing about their instruments and microphones. (See Billy Idol's "Rebel Yell," Scorpion's "Rock You Like a Hurricane," Van Halen's "Jump," Police's "Synchronicity," AC/DC's "For Those About to Rock, We Salute You.")

In nihilist videos, the love theme turns from a relatively mild narcissism and a focus on the pain of separation, to sadism, masochism, androgyny, and homoeroticism; while the anti-authority theme moves from mere unresolved Oedipal conflicts to explicit hate, nihilism, anarchy, destruction.

The nihilist video thus has (at least hitherto) taken up an angry, iconoclastic stance, making clear its position. The same has been true of the so-called "classical" video that is partly defined by its employing the traditional Hollywood "male" gaze toward the female figures. These are the videos that rely more than most others on narrative situations and that do not necessarily show band members performing with their instruments at all. The videos are however mainly "classical" in retaining the voyeuristic/fetishistic gaze toward woman as object of desire that feminist film theorists have spent so much time analyzing in relation to the classical Hollywood film.

61

These arguments are too well-known to be rehearsed here, and I will be returning to specific examples in the next chapter. But, briefly, these videos set up the female image as object of an obsessive male desire and are positioned in the male protagonist's viewpoint. There are numerous examples of this kind of video, but Rod Stewart's "Infatuation," John Parr's "Naughty Naughty," The Romantics' "Talking in Your Sleep," John Cougar's "Hurts so Good," The Rolling Stones' "She Was Hot," are familiar, oft-played examples. I'll be commenting later on the deliberately self-conscious stance toward their own voyeurism evident in these videos. (The Stewart video deliberately foregrounds the voyeurism in imaging the protagonist constantly photographing the desired woman, but the feature is perhaps at its most extreme in the popular David Lee Roth "California Girls" and "Just Like A Gigolo/I Ain't Got Nobody".) It is this self-consciousness that sets them off somewhat from the voyeurism in the classical film.

A second main "classical" type is that which derives largely from certain Hollywood film genres. Especially prevalent recently have been videos deriving from the horror, suspense, and science fiction film types. The type began relatively innocently with Jackson's famous "Thriller," but has lately gotten more ominous, as in Peter Gabriel's "Shock the Monkey," White Wolf's "Shadows in the Night," or Yes's "Owner of a Lonely Heart." In the Gabriel and White Wolf videos, some kind of alien presence inserts itself in the filmic world; in the first, it is a monkey that seems to cause the protagonist's strange alternation between his regular business self and a savage, totemic other self; in the latter, an alien presence enters the forest and frightens the young people away. The Yes video remains within the gangster tradition, as the protagonist is swept out of the mass of the people by rain-coated men in dark glasses, who submit him to a variety of tortures, physical and psychological. Duran Duran's "Wild Boys" also tends toward the science fiction mode: a group of men in some wrecked, post-holocaust world, tied to planks on a revolving wheel, seem to exist on the margins of civilization.

Powerful images of entrapment and unexplained descent evoke deep psychological fears in the viewer. While these are familiar from classical Hollywood genres, there is an important difference that again suggests the sliding over into postmodernism. For in most of the Hollywood genres mentioned here the mystery is ultimately resolved; we are given explanations (even if they involve "belief" in the possibility of extraterrestrial beings or in spirits/ghosts, etc.) for the events shown, so that the viewer leaves the cinema secure that he/she is living in a rational world. This is not the case for most of the videos described above: we never know why certain things happen, or even precisely what *is* happening. We are forced to exist in a non-rational, haphazard universe where we cannot expect any "closure" of the ordinary kind. On this level then, these so-called "classical" videos also gesture toward postmodernism.

What characterizes the postmodernist video is its refusal to take a clear position vis-à-vis its images, its habit of hedging along the line of not communicating a clear signified. In postmodernist videos, as not in the other specific types, each element of a text is undercut by others: narrative is undercut by pastiche; signifying is undercut by images that do not line up in a coherent chain; the text is flattened out, creating a two-dimensional effect and the refusal of a clear position for the spectator within the filmic world. This leaves him/her decentered, perhaps confused, perhaps fixated on one particular image or image-series, but most likely unsatisfied and eager for the next video where perhaps closure will take place.

Ambiguity of the image and frequency of pastiche is most evident in postmodern videos. These videos, which sometimes have loose narrative elements, are disturbing in not manifesting a position from which they speak; Motley Crue's "Too Young to Fall in Love," for example, has the trio – bizarrely dressed in tight leather pants, studded leather straps over bare chests, leather boots, and wearing their hair very long and straggly – involved in a James Bond-style oriental crime plot. With much macho maneuvering and improbable sword play, they rescue the beautiful young oriental girl from the clutches of her stolid fat captors. But it is impossible to tell whether or not this video intends to comment upon, and thus critique, the clichéd Bond conventions. Is it merely employing them for its own ends? Are we supposed to find interest in the contrast between the Bond mise-en-scène and the Motley Crue stars in their outlandish attire? Does the video merely want us to delight in the stars' wonderful, athletic bodies so highlighted by their clothes, and in their dazzling macho feats?

Queen's "Radio Ga Ga" is similarly difficult to read. In this case, an argument could be made for Queen self-consciously playing with images from Nazism and Germany in the 1930s, setting off Fritz Lang's version of the future (in footage taken from *Metropolis*) against futurist Star-Trek imagery. The intent then could be to link Lang's foreboding of fascism with the present. Supporting this view is the fact that the radio is recalled nostalgically as an instrument that pre-dated the dangerous proliferation of "spectacle" that Nazism so exploited and that contemporary youth celebrates in its very fascination with rock videos.

On the other hand, this reading is sophisticated and only possible within the framework of knowledge about Fritz Lang and fascism in 1930s Germany. The video does not itself construct a position for the spectator or even seem to raise questions about its own use of fascist imagery. It does not say whether it is for or against fascism, hedging along that line (mentioned above) of not letting us know what we are to do with images of proto-fascism. The rally scenes pastiche Leni Riefenstahl's *Triumph of the Will*, the figures looking like a cross between those in her film and in *Star-Trek*. The easy, regular beat of the music, with its haunting tune uncharacteristic of the postmodern type, is perhaps deliberately in opposition to the potential violence of the images, but the average spectator would not notice this ironic juxtaposition and is merely swept along in a way that is pleasurable rather than disjunctive or questioning. If there really *is* irony rather than pastiche, it takes work to grasp it.

The same is true of their recent "Princes of the Universe," which seems at once to parody and celebrate machismo and male acts of violence and destruction. The title might refer ironically to heads of powerful nations in the world, whose self-proclaimed omnipotence in fact leads to pathetic destruction (viz. the image of the child electrocuted as he hangs onto a bar). This is one of the videos with a futurist "look" that resembles a nuclear holocaust, and is packed with images of explosion and destruction. Yet the stars themselves appear to parade their power and virility as they withstand the onslaughts of their world, and seem to triumph over it. Again, the pastiche/satire boundary is blurred.

I have left the "socially conscious" video until last because I wish to focus on this type here. When I first started this work (and in some already published papers), I used the category to distinguish those videos which made social issues their specific theme from others which, following Althusser, are necessarily in ideology but do not have explicit ideological *content*. The "socially conscious" video is arguably the closest we have to one modernist tradition in western culture that deliberately positioned itself against the dominant bourgeois society. The great nineteenth-century novel produced one level of critique of bourgeois culture, followed by the post-romantic, modernist kind of critique. Although the category "modernism" is now under debate, it can still stand for a type of art that is in deliberate reaction against what are perceived as dominant, established forms. As a counter-art form, modernist texts defined themselves against what they opposed; this strand of modernism, then, was a largely *political* art, looking from a critical position, whether to the right or the left of the establishment.

From 1982 to 1985, one could find videos that still seemed ideologically linked to various forms of 1960s left and liberal humanism, i.e. that had behind them political signifieds embodied in on-going movements of certain kinds. These videos found their way onto MTV arguably because the station could not quite contain all positions shown during the 24-hour flow. So these "socially conscious" videos were there, albeit largely drowned out by the ongoing flow of the other types, and not usually cycled with any regularity.

In this sense, of course, the channel was not risking much in allowing the occasional video with politically liberal messages. Yet it is important that the format of short, four-minute texts permits gaps through which a variety of enunciative positions are possible. I am thus able to temporarily "stop the flow," in order to concentrate on representations other than the dominant postmodernist fixation on surfaces/textures/style/self-as-commodity that dominates the channel's offerings. But this is with full awareness that these isolated moments are overridden by the plethora of surrounding texts, and that this sort of focus only occurs within an academic discourse. These various possibilities for "seeing otherwise" are worth exploring in terms of understanding what popular culture *can* do, despite the fact that the average viewer will in fact have little opportunity for such alternate "seeing."

In the early 1980s, three themes dominated the "socially

John Cougar Mellencamp, "Authority"

In this "socially conscious" video, the protagonist is victimized by
representatives of authority.

conscious" video, all of which involve moments of disruption, conflict, rejection, and alienation. There were first the anti-parental, anti-authority videos, revealing adolescent disillusionment with, and distaste for, parental, work-related, or state authority. Protagonists are sometimes shown as painful victims of authority, as in John Cougar's "Authority Song" video, where the protagonist is victimized by all representatives of social authority; or that which equates Friday liberation from the work week with an escape from prison. Here, secretaries are imaged in chains that tie them to the desk, the boss (always fat and ugly) is bound up in ticker-tape by the liberators. The performers, in their anti-establishment punk clothes, are imaged as freedom fighters who destroy the office and the oppressors, releasing the employees.

The British have been most active in expressing a generalized, anti-establishment attitude that continues a tradition in British counter-culture dating from John Osborne's *Look Back in Anger* (1956) and embodied in the "Angry Young Man" movement that followed. Jo Boxer's "Just Got Lucky," which contrasts the happy-go-lucky band in their working-class men's clothes and box-cart, with a stuffy, over-weight and quarrelsome parental couple in their swanky car, was a typical early example of the type, as was also Stray Cats' "Look At That Cadillac." More explicitly anti-parental than anti-bourgeois, Mama's Boys' "Mama, We're All Crazy Now" shows a typical British working-class mother, busying herself doing housework for her son, suddenly catapulted into her son's rock and roll world when he arrives with his friends and starts loud, wild playing that nearly brings down the kitchen roof. The transition from the mother in the kitchen to the mother immersed in rock 'n roll is ironically conveyed through a Hitchcockian filmic moment, when we see only the mother's bedroom slippers creeping silently up the stairs to a certain kind of death.

Tears for Fears' "Mother's Talk" (in its third video version in 1986) operates on two levels simultaneously; it is again explicitly anti-parental (and anti-family), although the mother seems the most repressive figure in keeping with a long representational tradition.[6] But it makes this critique in the context of the sudden outbreak of nuclear war; that is, we see the pathetic/stupid reactions of a working class family (circa early 1950s), with Moma at the ironing board, head-cloth and apron in place, Dad reading the paper, boy on the floor watching a TV set on which images of a hydrogen bomb exploding (the start of the nuclear holocaust) alternate with those of the band in performance. Mother is seen berating boy, who ignores her, when suddenly the father realizes from watching the TV what is happening, and begins to dismantle doors and to paint over the windows in an effort to build the "inner refuge" the TV demonstrates. The mother, meanwhile, tries to hoover up the father, increasing his rage. The video ends with the onset of a nuclear war and the family packing all their belongings; they wave to the camera, from their obviously inadequate "refuge," as the video ends.

The Kinks' imaginative and poignant "Do It Again" and Wham!'s more aggressive "Bad Boys" exemplify the kind of video that has been coming from England recently, as does also the Dream Academy's "Life in a Northern Town," with its poignant, nostalgic look back at the 1960s and John F. Kennedy and the Beatles. The videos all have an explicit working-class identification and a clear anti-middle-class point of view: the political codes that structure the position within British society are evident, and provide a kind of referent *behind* the text.

Some American bands picked up the stance in 1985, but partly because class codes function very differently here from Britain, and partly because by 1985 there was already a sliding over into the postmodern stance in which social themes exist *merely* as representations and lack any political referents any more, the results are startlingly different. Sammy Hagar's "I Can't Drive at 55," and Motley Crue's "Smokin' in the Boys' Room" are representative of what is going on in America. Let me briefly analyze this latter comic video so as to provide some sense of the "new" anti-authority position.

"Smokin' in the Boys' Room", in pastiching a 1974 Brownsville station song, is a postmodern version of the socially conscious video. Its comedy works through the relationship between song and image, and through play with a kind of Bakhtinian notion of the carnivalesque, particularly as this has been discussed recently by Peter Stallybrass and Allon White.[7] Like much of MTV, the usage of past modes is superficial – textural rather than fully ideological; but, in Bakhtin's words, Motley Crue's video does celebrate "temporary liberation from the prevailing truth of the established order," and marks "the suspension of all hierarchical rank, privileges, norms and prohibitions." For Bakhtin, "Carnival was the true feast of time, the feast of becoming, change and renewal, it was hostile to all that was immortalized and complete."[8] Certain American bands like Motley Crue (one could also include Twisted Sister, Ozzy Osbourne, Kiss, and others) play with the carnivalesque in their anti-establishment videos, perhaps replacing political protest against the established order with a kind of "licensed release" arguably characteristic of the carnival.[9]

"Smokin' in the Boys' Room" carries us quickly and efficiently through the establishing narrative (the hero loses his homework, is sent to the Principal and whipped and retires to the boys' room to recover). The musical instruments – and sound effects, such as the dog's growl, the slamming doors, the rushing noise as Jimmy approaches the Principal, the sound of the whip, etc. – effectively underscore the humorous camera work used for Jimmy and the teachers (wide-angle lenses, high angle shots, extreme close-ups, etc.). Jimmy looks into the mirror and, echoing the Principal (who had bemoaned the fact that Jimmy was "Never able to see *our* side of things"), wonders why "Somebody can't see *my* side of it."

At this point, Jimmy suddenly sees the images of the four Motley Crue band members in the mirror; one of them pops his head out, and tells Jimmy that they have found a way of getting out of the world of authority. Combining the carnivalesque tradition outlined by Bakhtin with more recent 1960s concepts, this world, when viewed from the "other" side of the mirror, is now seen to be "crazy." Values are turned upside down: what was before "rational" authority is now exposed as repressive and inhibiting. The band members pull the boy across into the world of the grotesque in which all bourgeois restraints are released. From here, Jimmy looks out at the school world transformed into madness and horror from the alternate, carnivalesque position.

To begin with, the band's own clothes are a total (and radical) violation of normal male dress clothes. Three of the band members (the drummer remains seated throughout) are dressed in even more outlandish get-ups than usual: the point seems to be to shock the establishment by the blurring of the usual male/female dress barrier – a familiar element in the carnival. Motley Crue all have very long

Motley Crue, "Smokin' in the Boys' Room"

Motley Crue, "Home Sweet Home"

The point is to mock the establishment by blurring usual male/female dress codes.

hair, elaborately styled, faces made up to look like women, with long eyelashes, heavy lipstick, mascara, rouge, etc.; they wear earrings and necklaces and have painted nails. Their clothes are also feminine, one of them wearing a one-piece suit, with dots on it, golden epaulettes and wide sash; another, white sequined pants, shiny necklace, a huge sequined belt, amulets, bracelets, a low-cut sleeveless top, and patches over crotch and rear; a third wears short leather pants and high leather boots, and a leather jacket with cut pieces, *gamin* style. Halfway through the video, they change clothes, one now wearing a white and black striped imitation of coat-tails, another a long leopard-skin coat and boots. The clothes in themselves are enough to disrupt the "straight" world on the other side of the mirror; far more than the 1960s "hippies," Motley Crue draw upon traditions of the medieval and renaissance clown, as well as upon more recent conventions of the transvestite.

But the group have other telling secrets to reveal: from the other side, the regular classroom looks like a jail, with a Nazi-style lady warden in charge (shades of Lina Wertmuller's Commandant in *Seven Beauties*); the students are all hooked up to machines, their faces and eyes fastened so that they have to look directly at a bright light (one recalls Plato's cave allegory here). Since students might manage to use one eye to look elsewhere, the warden patrols the machines, controlling all with a huge gear on which the word "Conform" is written in large letters.

Meanwhile, Motley Crue reveal the stupidity and inanity of the Principal, who is associated with a look-alike puppet. The band disrupts the ever-vigilant video camera, which, like Foucault's Panopticon, allows students to be seen without themselves seeing. The band first put a picture of their Other Side world in front of the camera, but then allow their own images to appear on the Principal's multi-screens, much to his dismay. They walk Jimmy into the auditorium, where the music teacher is performing, push him off the stage, and take over, to the wild delight of the students.

After a liberating and hectic performance, students dancing madly to the music, Motley Crue return Jimmy to the boys' room whence they took him. The Principal offers an apology, now scorned by Jimmy, who winks at his friends in the mirror, and pulls off the Principal's wig, revealing his ugly, egg-shaped head.

71

ROCKING AROUND THE CLOCK

The inventive music track for this video, together with the group's extraordinary appearance, enables the whole to transcend its narrative clichés. The musical sounds in the opening section used to indicate the brutality and inhumanity of the school are effective, and throughout the instruments create a hard-driving, heavy metal sound that perfectly suits the comic turns of the plot. The band's music defines the "other side" as much as anything else, and seems to embody the carefree, iconoclastic stance of the rebels. But the visuals also add a good deal: the idea of contrasting the straight and subversive worlds through the device of the mirror is imaginative and effective. It provides a graphic visual correlative for the concept, and permits a constant play with the notion of "seeing" and "being seen," but in far different terms from the standard Hollywood shot/counter-shot cutting sequence. The rebels look out onto, and thereby manage to control, and ultimately conquer, the world of the establishment. The video supports the idea that "liberation" lies through rock sounds and through refusing to conform to essentially moribund (if not corrupt), stuffy, bourgeois values. But, unlike the genuine Bakhtinian carnival, the protest remains superficial: mere play with oppositional signifiers rather than a protest that emerges from a powerful class and community base.

These generalized anti-establishment videos seem largely the province of male stars, and rarely even include reference to women, unless they are of the fat/ugly types to be ridiculed (as in "Smokin' in the Boys' Room"). Motley Crue's feminized appearance seems rather to mark the absence of women as something desirable. They have incorporated the feminine, as it were, making its actual presence superfluous. The band takes the place of women in Jimmy's life, while vicariously providing the semblance of the feminine. This sort of androgynous address, common in nihilist videos, will be more fully explored later on.

It might also be noted, briefly, that the American anti-establishment videos differ from the British ones in their clichéd ridicule of generalized (not class-marked) authority figures. The British seem rather to follow the tradition (immortalized by the Beatles) of exposing the pathos and banality of the routine, daily bourgeois life that people are tracked into without their being aware of what is happening to them. Sometimes the British try to show such people as stupid (as in the Kinks' video referred to), but often they will be empathetic. Sometimes they delight in being different, but are just as likely to express a certain poignancy about their alienation from the crowd. At any rate, by and large, the British anti-establishment videos are not so aggressively machismo as many of the American ones.

Perhaps the best socially conscious videos of a general kind on the American scene are the rare ones that fit into what we might call the "art" or "avant-garde" video. (That this type is finally being recognized as such by the channel is evident in the creation of a new slot, "The New Video Hour," perhaps inspired by the Newark-based Channel U-68.) The well-known Polish video director, Zbigniew Rybczynski, often produces videos of this type, as for instance in his "Close to the Edit" for Art of Noise, or his "Sign of the Times" for Grandmaster Flash. He is best known, perhaps, for his work with Simple Minds. For their recent "All the Things She Said," Rybczynski used a digital disk video recorder that allowed him to shoot and

Peter Gabriel, "Sledgehammer"

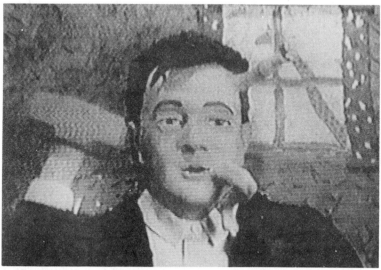

In this extraordinarily creative video, no objects remain what they seem for long: the video is constructed around the idea of *transformation*.

edit simultaneously. This breakthrough in video technology made possible a continuous flow of 112 separate takes, all slightly different. Also interesting are experimental videos by Sly Fox (another black and white team) called "Let's Go All the Way"; or any by the extraordinary artist Grace Jones. Peter Gabriel's disturbing "Sledgehammer" is yet another example of a creative use of the video form. Here Gabriel's face is filmed in stop-motion technique to produce a disorienting, jerky series of images, and the instability of objects becomes the norm; one thing is transmuted into another, often grotesque, form, until at the end even the human body turns into a series of shapes that dissolve into the cosmos, there now being merely an infinite, boundless, and inhuman universe. The Art of Noise's "Paranoimia," featuring as it does the computerized man, or "simulacrum," similarly addresses the confusion of boundary between human/non-human of an advanced technological era.

But the Talking Heads' "Burning Down the House" and Laurie Anderson's rarely shown "Language is a Virus" are both more obviously socially conscious examples. The creative use of metaphor in "Burning Down the House," and the aesthetic intelligence underlying the video's construction, typify much of David Byrne's work. Here the trope of "house" can be taken in the senses of both the historical subject and of the public sphere; it works on both levels at once, suggesting the archaism and inadequacy of the family as an institution, while also implying that the State no longer has the ability to create a meaningful society. The symbolic sub-urban house dominates the video as an image constantly returned to; its side wall (facing the camera) functions like a screen on which different images are projected (Byrne's haunted face, blown up large; flames; the concert audience with the search light panning across them, suggesting hostile authority over people). The performers themselves symbolize family members, Byrne's child self alternating with his adult one. At one point the various faces of the family members superimpose themselves on one another, representing the aim of family life to shape its members in one mould, "Everything stuck together," as the lyric notes. At another point, the band members mimic the burden family members impose on one another by climbing on each other's backs while the words on the track note, "I don't know what you expect of me." The final images suggest isolation and fragmentation, as we see Byrne's back, apparently facing emptiness rather than people; and his disconnected face superimposed over a panning shot of an empty road. Throughout, the staccato words and the deliberately mechanically orchestrated beat, together with the blank faces and robot-like movements of the performers, convey the sense of a world devoid of, and disillusioned with, earlier familiar comforts.

Laurie Anderson's "Language is a Virus" constructs an equally alienated environment; Anderson relies on staccato phrasing and robot-like gestures not unlike Byrne's.[10] In addition, at times her musicians wear stocking-masks over their faces, and strange, lamp-like headgear. Godardian fashion, Anderson uses words floating across her image to underscore and add meanings, and the whole is well-edited on movement and music beat. Taking her theme from a William Burroughs quotation, "Language is a virus from outer space," Anderson uses a combination of cinematic images, avant-garde theatre, computer graphics, play with the TV and cinema screens, all held together by her own half-talking voice, commenting on the abuses of language that in turn lead to exploitation (particularly of woman by man, it seems).

A second theme in "socially conscious" videos has been more specific allusion to foreign policy or specific social injustices, such as poverty. Again, the British bands lead the way, and they alone retain much of the genuinely political era of rock and roll (1967-70). These explicitly resisting videos are, however, very rarely shown on MTV. Frankie Goes to Hollywood's powerful "Two Tribes" video, which makes a bitter comment about East—West relations with specific reference to Ronald Reagan and the Soviet leader – we see the two aging men wrestling in a circus ring – was shown very infrequently, but it makes just the kind of ironic comment likely to reach viewers. The Clash and other rebellious British bands get scant attention from the channel.

Perhaps influenced by the British, there has recently (1986) been a significant increase in the explicitly political video on MTV. Let me deal with four examples in some detail. First, there is the sort of generalized critique of an America seen through the eyes of a Vietnam veteran, as in Bruce Springsteen's "Born in the USA." This represents a genuine outraged reaction to social conditions and the

Vietnam War, and the political referents are obvious. Second, there is the less politically explicit and more visually experimental stance of a band like Midnight Oil, whose "Best of Both Worlds" is an ironic comment on the state of things, in the general mode of Frankie Goes to Hollywood. Third, I want to attend briefly to a heavy metal band, Sammy Hagar, whose "V.O.A." indicates that the right can also make political videos, if again veering off in the postmodernist direction. Finally, there is the recent spate of videos inspired by the "USA/Africa" event/video, which has been influential in making concern for the starving fashionable. While Springsteen was influential in this as in the related "Sun-City" video to be discussed below, he should not be seen as responsible for the, perhaps, postmodernist result of these efforts. Springsteen is personally unusual in the American rock scene in seeming to retain genuine identification with the working class and the generally "oppressed" of this world.

Springsteen's hard-driving video, "Born in the USA," reflects the

Bruce Springsteen, "Born in the USA"

Springsteen's "ironic" patriotism: here the star turns his head away from the (suggested) American flag

76

bitter irony common to many songs on the "USA" album. The first part of the video focuses mainly on Springsteen himself, in performance, yelling the song words into the microphone. His deep, husky voice and angry, rebellious face and body mimic the hard-driving, loud, repetitive beat of the music. The camera stays close-in on his face most of the time, revealing his 1960s style bandana, long hair, and army jacket. Occasionally, we pull back to his full figure, with arm raised in angry protest, fans' arms also waving in front frame. The words, shouted rather than sung, tell how the hero "Got in a little hometown jam" and was sent "to a foreign land to go and kill the yellow man." This is followed by a long series of repeated lines "Born in the USA," while the visuals show largely different close-ups of Springsteen's face.

The next section of the song and video tells of the return home to work in a refinery and of the Vet Man's inability to help. There are images here recalling the hero's happy childhood in a working-class neighborhood; he is seen at a birthday party, in a high school photo, on his bike, going off to a wedding.

We cut back to Springsteen on stage where again we have close-ups of his face as he repeats the "Born in the USA" lines again several times. This dissolves to images of fairground cars, followed by two possible "adult" cars – a fancy, sleek car and an old, decorated car, "For Sale." This is followed by a similar series of ironic contrasts that reflect American life – the welfare men standing outside a "Checks Cashed" place; a young man firing a gun at a fairground, which dissolves to American soldiers in a jungle in Vietnam surrendering to the enemy; followed by a close-up of a vet with one blinded eye, to other vets with tattoos on the arm, which dissolves to images of soldiers fighting in Vietnam, and again dissolves to pick up a tiny Vietnamese child walking on a street. As the music blares, Springsteen's voice rises to a cry, and the child-image dissolves into a fast-moving camera panning the rows and rows of white graves at Arlington Cemetery, ending in a dissolve to Springsteen's screaming face on the stage. We cut to images of men working in a welding factory as the long-held screaming note continues. On a flare of light in the factory, the video returns to the stage, to pick up Springsteen's band members – the drummer, the guitarist, hectically playing on that same high note, the fans screaming away in audience.

Bruce Springsteen, "Glory Days"

Bruce Springsteen, "I'm On Fire"

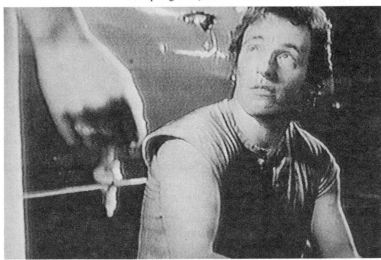

Springsteen's social consciousness is evident in other videos: "Glory Days" images
the star in a working-class bar; "I'm On Fire" stresses the class discrepancy that
inhibits the romance. The absence of the woman's face, and her fragmented body
indicate her Symbolic status as lack, absent desire.

78

THE FIVE TYPES OF VIDEO

The video ends on a quieter, but still ironic note, showing images of young people – a young girl hard-hat, a girl on a bike, black performers, a man drinking coke, school girls walking home, men playing baseball – that is, shots of daily American life that still goes on, heedless of the meaningless pain and death in Vietnam. It is in fact the ironic juxtaposition of images that makes the song's already powerful statement even more so. Springsteen's musical score, in turn, reinforces both visuals and words in its loud, angry, rebellious sounds; it is as if the instruments are screaming out their rage at the way things are, echoing the hero's rage. Being "Born in the USA," that is, means being born to a senseless killing and to involving oneself in battle, injury, and death that belies happy childhood hopes and fantasies. Springsteen's recent "War" video, from his new *Live* album, reinforces and takes further themes in "Born in the USA."

Midnight Oil's "Best of Both Worlds" is in a vein rather similar to the Springsteen video, only perhaps with more humor in the bitter irony. The band present themselves in quite unconventional manner, the lead having a totally bald head, and the others dressed in various working-men's clothes. The video again consists of intercutting between the band in concert and images taken from newsreel footage, but there is a third space in this video – that of the outerspace from which the men look back on, and comment upon, doings on earth.

The first section shows the men in concert: the stage is dark, and they are lit in film noir fashion, so that they loom as spots in amongst the shadows. The music is hard-driving, unmelodious and, like Springsteen, the members shout rather than sing their words. As the music starts, we get shots of the men leaping about the stage in slow motion; there is quick intercutting between different band members, the film footage merely superimposed on the sound, and the camera is often so close in that we are not sure what we are seeing. As the song starts, the lead is filmed with an outerspace background, in which worlds are seen turning around. The first theme lines, "Times are tough/We got the best of both worlds," are repeated as we get a series of newsreel footage images – a rocket going off, a third world child dying, an image of Reagan's cheerful face, an image of a third world adult in the throes of death – first the body, then facial close-up; a shot of soldiers firing, a shot of the

United States of America with major towns lit up, a shot of prisoners behind barbed wire, shortly juxtaposed ironically with a shot of
fans' arms waving in a manner similar to that of the prisoners; a
shot of another rocket taking off, and then of women and children
on a third world, war-torn street.

We return to a sequence of shots of the band members, still singing the lines "Times are tough/We got the best of both worlds," followed by a repeat of war images and the rocket already seen. The
next section changes somewhat to show the leader of the band floating in outerspace, from where he comments on the "real" world not
being as good as it could have been. The music reaches its most loud,
insistent, angry heights as these latter words are sung, over and over.
The final image takes a comic stance, showing the band members on
the moon, trying to catch the sausages they've cooked that constantly
float away.

Both these videos make demands on the spectator not usual in
rock videos on MTV. They do not construct an easy position for the
viewer, and rely on viewers bringing certain reading formations to
reception. For instance, how/where is the viewer supposed to identify? The stars are in so angry, rebellious a mood that identification
with them is difficult, although I think this is what the spectator has
to do; the newsreel footage moves fast, and the precise images can
only be grasped on repeated viewings (stopping and pausing to get
the full shot). The viewer is being barraged with information which
is, however, imprecise. The decoding is not easy. The full meaning
of the videos can only be understood if one deliberately thinks about
what has been shown, which is not necessary for instance in the
other types to be examined in the next chapter. The various pleasurable kinds of gaze that I'll also discuss there do not come into play
here; one is forced, Brechtian style, to the more distanced position
of watching and listening and thinking about what is going on. It is
possible, however, that the insistent beat of the music, the energy,
vitality, and clear commitment to express something considered
important, can simply sweep the viewer along. The images and the
music move fast, so that one's sensory organs are kept busy, even if
one does not have time or inclination to think about what it all
means.

A very different relationship to the status quo, this time from a heavy metal group, can be found in Sammy Hagar's "V.O.A." (i.e. "Voice of America"). Someone seeing the video from the perspective of liberal-humanist reading formations might be tempted to read the video as parody, but ultimately it is clear that it is closer to propaganda for "Voice of America" than a comic critique. Although there is comic play with both the standard Hollywood James Bond-style spy movie, and the international manipulations of the CIA, the video ends up celebrating "terrorist-style rockers" who are really vigilantes.

Hagar and the band members represent themselves as macho-style terrorist "rockers" aiding in CIA international dealings. The video begins with Hagar telling the enemy diplomat whom he has kidnapped, in no uncertain terms, that "We got to fight/Let's make that clear/If you push too hard/You're going to fall"; as these words are sung, we cut to shots of a gun battle between men in the hero's car and the pursuing enemy. Throughout the video, Hagar shouts rather than sings his words, and the heavy metal music keeps up a fast, loud pace; drums figure largely in the composition, while the guitars whine and scream as if to underscore the angry, patriotic stance of the protagonists, who, full of boundless energy, are determined to win.

As Hagar screams "We got fifty million rockers/All with guns," we cut to shots of men in black outfits, firing their guns from an open truck. At this point the group sing the macho-style lines, "We don' like it/We won't take it/Let it rock," that are repeated at intervals. The next section, in Damascus, shows the CIA and the Russians trading secrets, as Hagar sings "We're trying to strike/Everybody knows." As the music plays, we see Hagar avoiding capture because his group, in disguise, open fire and save him. We cut to Hagar looking through the film he's taken from a camera inside a false tooth, as he tells us "When we're together/We're the best/We think as one/There's no contest." Hagar claims "We got the power/They know the score," just before, ironically, he is finally captured and thrown into a rat- and insect-ridden cell. The words now cease as the music takes over for an interlude that shows the complexity of the composition and the skillful use of instruments to make interesting and fitting sounds. The sequence of the enemy's dragging Hagar to the electric chair and trying to make him talk is cut so as to coincide with the rhythm of the music; the sounds furthermore parallel what we see going on in the images, reaching their height at the moment of Hagar's attempted electrocution. In fact, he magically breaks free, runs off, and is next seen driving his car. His voice picks up the musical line on a long-held scream "No-o-o-o-o-," before the band chime in with the refrain, Hagar's voice rising above with the same "No-o-o-o."

In the final sequence, the music rises to fever pitch as we return to the opening car gun-battle, some images repeated from the earlier scene, and witness the protagonists' triumph over the enemy. The group now chant "Voice of America" several times, to underscore their patriotism. The last images are of the car blowing up in a huge explosion. Flames fill the screen as the camera follows the smoke up into the sky.

The vigilante violence evident in this video is a disturbing sign of the times. In other words, one can no longer assume that "rockers" are liberal humanists. The violence and anarchism of the nihilist video is here meshed with patriotic vigilante ideology involving direct action for the establishment in a united front. The political "referents" are here clear, although the comic mode still suggests a certain distance on Hagar's part toward what he is proclaiming.

None of these videos, whether from the right or the left, are frequently cycled on MTV and, except for the Springsteen, the stars are less well known. This has partly to do with MTV's commercial concern to keep things politically "safe"; but there is also the general Reaganite American climate that the channel addresses because that is where its audience is at. As John Orman notes, in a recent book on *The Politics of Rock Music*, the Gallup Youth Survey of 1977 "captured the sad state of rock in music by surveying 1069 teenagers in a random sample."[11] The list of top twenty artists selected by the teenagers in 1977 did not include "a true political rocker among them." According to Orman, "Rock had grown lazy and tame in all of its overblown opulence; it was hardly on the cutting edge of society change. Rock stars had to pay for their homes on the West Coast, the drugs, the limousines, and the good times. American popular culture easily absorbed the rock star into its class structure."

In the 1980s, Orman evidently conducted his own small survey and found little correlation between a person's favorite rock star and political attitudes. His sample (from a private Jesuit institution) all ranked USA, Jesus Christ, Catholics, and Martin Luther King, Jr, high; communists, homosexuals, blacks, the USSR, low. Of the fans, grouped into three based on their choice of Jackson Browne, Bruce Springsteen or punk/new wave music as their favorite kind, the punk/new wave were the least conservative, the Jackson Browne the most, with Springsteen in between.

A recent *Newsweek* article suggests the same general conservatism among rock fans and points out the irony of Bruce Springsteen's vast following, evidently not lost on Springsteen himself. According to *Newsweek*, Springsteen is imaged as an "all American guy" – a "kind of American archetype." He is "rock and roll's Gary Cooper – a simple man who expresses strong beliefs with passion and unquestioned sincerity. He is rock and roll's Jimmy Cagney as well – streetwise and fiery, a galvanic mixture of body and soul." Leery of being an icon, Springsteen sees such hero worship as antipathetic to rock's originally rebellious stance. Ironically, fans evidently take Springsteen's "Born in the USA" as "an exultant anthem for Reagan-era America."[12]

It would be impossible to mistake the message in a rare anti-Vietnam video which used newsreel footage from the war to expose the suffering and extreme youth of the men involved. Or that of The Firm's "Live in Peace," which implicates all nations in continuing hostilities that seem to be leading to world-wide destruction. Aside from the gratuitous imaging of evil in the clichéd forms of woman and snake, the video makes its point about the gap between government and ordinary people, who simply want to live in peace, well. Equally direct and earnest is John Cougar Mellencamp's "Rain on the Scarecrow" made in direct response to the plight of farmers in spring 1986, who were increasingly forced by desperate economic plight to give up land that had been in their families for generations. Jackson Browne's "For America," very much in the Springsteen mode, at once celebrates the high democratic American ideal – America's rhetoric about freedom – while deploring the failure to live up to the ideal. "The freedom I found," he sings, "Wasn't quite as free when the truth was known." The lyric and the images express at once loyalty and love for America, and profound disillusionment and distress at the automatic "my country right or wrong" stance of many, and at America's having lost its conscience. The greatest and the most ignoble images of America's recent history are spliced together in an effective documentary-style montage.

But these videos are rare on MTV, only played at best a few times; otherwise, the closest MTV videos come to anything like a political referent are those like Don Henley's "All She Wants to do is Dance." Set in a guerrilla-warfare context, the focus of this video, despite the setting, is on the craziness of a young, perhaps shell-shocked girl, who, disregarding the street fighting going on around her, only wants to dance. (The sexist assumption that the girl cannot get involved in the political scene is typical of "political" videos.)

From this perspective, the recent USA Africa event/video, followed by the International "Live Aid" effort that brought together rock stars from America, Britain, Europe, and even the Soviet Union in a joint project to raise money for people starving in Ethiopia, seemed an encouraging sign of youth's concern with anything going on in the public sphere. While not exactly a radical cause, the two projects apparently demonstrated that rock stars could put aside their narcissistic interests in the service of something larger than themselves. The video and the Live Aid live transmission gave spectators a sense of being part of a community brought together around a moral cause unrelated to direct self-interest. The events incited a moral feeling in young people in an unusual way, and this can only be to the good. In addition, the fact that the Live Aid event (which involved thousands of young people at all-day-long concerts in London and Philadelphia) came off without any violence or disruptions showed a far different climate from that of the early 1970s, when rock had gone sour and when events like Altamont took place.

Further fundraising and consciousness-raising events around social issues followed those directed at poverty in Africa: the "Sun-City" video (in which again Springsteen played an important role) tackled the apartheid issue, on the heels of student campus protests, making a strong anti-apartheid statement; there was a Fashion Video event geared toward victims of Aids and several videos were made about the deadly disease (although they did not appear on MTV, as far as I am aware). Most recently, there was a Farm Aid Event in which rock, jazz, and folk stars participated. As noted, John

THE FIVE TYPES OF VIDEO

Cougar Mellencamp has made a striking video about the plight of the farmers near his home town, "Rain on the Scarecrow." It begins with a documentary-style interview with farmers describing their losses, and then moves into a visual essay on the pitiful conditions to which many American farmers have been reduced.

These events are interesting precisely because they took place within MTV's overarching commercial framework. Within that framework, one could obviously not expect in-depth political analysis to accompany events or to be embodied within the videos. It is certainly meaningful that young people are taking any kind of moral stand for those less fortunate than themselves. But what interests me about the videos and the events is the way that the organizers' genuine and committed intentions are taken up in the televisual apparatus and turned, inevitably, into something else. That is, it was hard to prevent these events turning into *media* events, hard to stop the televisual apparatus itself becoming the *event*. In the Live Aid event particularly, focus was on the awesome technological achievement of cross-Atlantic and inter-continental transmissions at the expense of the *cause* behind the events.

Likewise, it was hard to prevent events from becoming showcases for the stars — for *who* was to be there taking precedence over *why* everyone was there. Emphasis slipped over into the self-sacrifices the stars were making in time and money to be at the events (much, for instance, was made of Phil Collins's physical feat in performing first at the Wembley Stadium in London and then flying Concorde-speed to play in Philadelphia), and while this provides a useful model of moral behavior generally, it does not particularly publicize the problems of poverty and starvation, or give us better understanding of the political issues involved.

The question is complex in that indeed the stars' presence did attract millions of people and result in millions of dollars of donations. But the narcissistic elements were inevitably there on the part of both stars and audience. One cannot say that one gave one's money more for the stars than for the Ethiopians, but it is that very intermingling of issues, that blurring of boundaries between narcissistic desire and disinterested concern for the Other that seems postmodern.

Baudrillard has addressed this issue in his essays "In the Shadow of the Silent Majorities," and " . . . Or the End of the Social." In the first, Baudrillard notes that "Immense energy is expended in mitigating the tendentially declining rate of political investment and the absolute fragility of the social principle of reality, in maintaining this simulation of the social."[13] This notion is picked up and developed in the second essay, where Baudrillard talks of the "task of all media" as that of producing the "real, this extra real (interviews, live coverage, movies, TV-Truth, etc.)" (p. 84). For Baudrillard, the collapse of the distance between the real and its representation "puts an end to the real as referential by exalting it as a model" (p. 85). The real is "trapped in its own 'blown up' and desperate staging, in its own obscenity" (p. 85).

As always, Baudrillard seems to be onto some truth but, carried away by the force of his own rhetoric, to take it too far. Yet an occasional video, like Jimmy Barnes's "Working Class Man," would seem to fit his sense that actual political referents no longer exist: this video images so-called "working-class" men of all nationalities, taking off (presumably) from people like Springsteen and Mellencamp, but without situating the workers in any specific way. The video seems to bemoan the raw deal that working men get, yet there is no explanation for why they are so positioned. They are, then, reduced to mere signifiers, with which the video plays, and are not linked to any signifieds that would make a coherent statement.

In addition, the Live Aid and other media events, such as the "Hands Across America," suggest the effort to "simulate the social" of which Baudrillard talks. In this light, it is perhaps not surprising that "USA Africa" got the most airplay of all social issue videos, since it permits viewers at once to experience an unspecific, sentimentalized feeling of pity for the poor, together with an uplifting sense of wanting to be part of making "a better world," *and* to delight in close-up shots of their favorite stars. The video elicits the response "Oh, so-and-so's over there," or "Look at Michael Jackson who dressed up anyway," or "Isn't Bruce *fantastic*?" The song's catchy tune was important in bringing in the viewer and in making the experience pleasurable, but any specific information about poverty – even in dramatic images – was entirely absent.

The anti-apartheid video was rather different because, as in the case of the later Farm Aid Event, the politics behind the event were more

86

THE FIVE TYPES OF VIDEO

Artists Against Apartheid, "Sun City"

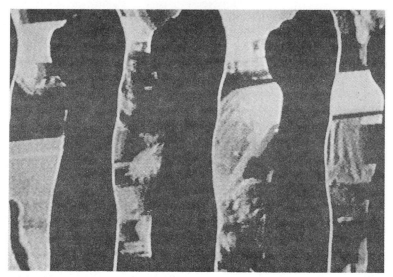

This video makes a strong anti-apartheid statement, sometimes by using
graphics and posters.

specific. By the time of the "Sun-City" video, young Americans had
become quite involved with anti-apartheid activities, persuading
universities to give up their stocks in South African corporations (or
ones investing in South Africa) through dramatic demonstrations
and the erection of "shanty-houses" on campuses. Perhaps because
of this, the video focused much more than did "USA Africa" on the
politics involved, at least in the sense of the abuses of apartheid. The
contrast between the pleasure-seeking white ruling classes and the
poor, ill-housed blacks, deprived of many basic rights, is illustrated
through the swift montage sequences of shots, some still photographs, interspersed among images of the rebellious, angry crowd
demonstrating against apartheid. Springsteen's image is captured,
but not obsessively so. In this video, the focus is deliberately on the
people, not the stars.

The final theme in the socially conscious video is women's oppression and the possibilities for female solidarity. Since Chapter 5 will
deal with the ideology of gender in select videos by male and female

87

stars, with the representation of the female body and with the various kinds of "gaze" videos construct, it seems more appropriate to include the so-called "feminist" videos in that discussion.

5

Gender address and the gaze in MTV

As we have already seen, the very existence of different gazes and gender address on MTV, arising as they do from the specificities of the televisual apparatus already discussed and from the cultural codes governing America today, is part of what marks MTV as a postmodernist phenomenon. Thematically and aesthetically the videos gather up into themselves the previously distinct art modes, with their corresponding iconography, world views, myths, ideologies, specific techniques; they create out of western cultural history a kind of grab-bag to dip into at will, obliterating historical specificity. Correspondingly, the channel refuses to construct just one dominant gender address as did previous art movements and genres. It rather constructs several different kinds of gender address and modes of representing sexuality, several different positions for the spectator to take up in relation to sexual difference.

As we also saw earlier, one of the still unresolved issues in Television Studies is the degree to which film theories can apply to very different televisual apparatus.[1] Since feminist film theory has emerged from a study of the classical Hollywood film, it is important for women approaching television to consider how far that theory is relevant to the different apparatus that television is. We need particularly to explore how far theories of the "male gaze" apply to watching television: if the apparatus itself produces certain inevitable "narrative" effects, such as in film the forced identification

89

with the (arguably male) look of the camera, we need to know how the televisual apparatus constructs the female body, and how bound by the limits of the apparatus are the images of women on TV.

MTV once again provides an ideal site for studying such questions since it carries to an extreme, as already noted, the linear flow of relatively short text-segments of different kinds inherent to the televisual apparatus. The apparatus, as a result, seems not to be gender specific in its very mode of functioning in the manner of the Hollywood film. Across its various segments TV in general, and MTV in particular, constructs a variety of gazes that indicate address to a certain kind of male or female imaginary. I will argue that there is sometimes a genderless address, and also that people of both genders undertake multiple identifications, depending on what particular video is being shown.

The plethora of gender positions on the channel is arguably linked to the heterogeneity of current sex roles and to an imaginary constructed out of a world in which all traditional categories, boundaries, and institutions are being questioned. The androgynous surface of many star images indicates the blurring of clear lines between genders characteristic of many rock videos, and which I'll address later on. All of this is linked to what I have been calling the increasing movement of rock videos into the postmodern stance, in which it is unclear what position a text is taking toward what it shows. This has implications for gender in that one often cannot tell whether a male or a female discourse dominates, and because the attitude toward sex and gender is often ambiguous. As I already mentioned, even in the category that I call "classical" because of its voyeuristic male gaze, there may be a studied self-consciousness that makes the result quite different from that in dominant commercial cinema. For instance, one finds oneself not quite knowing whether a video like John Parr's "Naughty Naughty" or Cougar Mellencamp's "Hurts So Good" is virulently sexist or merely pastiching an earlier Hollywood sexism.

In order to situate the forthcoming discussions, let me summarize briefly what feminist film theorists have argued about the cinema. According to these theories, the cinema as an apparatus at once evokes, and then attempts to resolve, original traumas around the Mother as sexual object. For the male spectator, arguably, it is at once the illicit desire for the mother and the fear of sexual difference (her castration) that the classical Hollywood film seeks to bring under control. But in so doing, it first evokes the original illicit erotic pleasure in sex with the parent.

In this theory, then, the female image on film functions rather as sign for something in the male unconscious than as anything to do with the historical female subject. The cinematic gaze is largely a *male* gaze, relying on Freud's twin mechanisms of voyeurism and fetishism as devices for the male spectator to avoid the threat that woman offers. "Woman" is then figured in three main ways: first, as ideal asexual mother, transcendent and nurturing the hero; second, as fetishized object, when the woman is given phallic attributes to lessen her threat (virtually presented as non-male rather than as "female"); or, third, woman is degraded by a voyeuristic gaze, her body set up as mere object of sexual desire, having no intrinsic meaning.[2]

Limited aspects of Lacan, as was discussed earlier, further created an analogy between the mirror and the screen; film-going was now seen as producing a regression to the Lacanian mirror phase, when the child saw a more perfect body than he in fact possessed, creating a split-subjectivity. This ideal imago is reproduced for the male spectator in the male heroes who dominate the landscape and control the narrative in the main male film genres.

Much of this work is now being modified, both in terms of paying more attention to the female spectator's position, and of realizing that gender address is far more complicated than the original model implies. Scholars have begun to work on the idea that multiple identifications take place for both male and female spectators through the narrative process, and on the notion that the pre-Oedipal as well as the Oedipal phase may be important in film spectatorship.[3]

But even so, theories have to start from the mechanisms of dominant classical Hollywood cinema that, as we've seen, rely on suturing the spectator into the image-sequence, on shot/counter-shot constructions, on the 180 degree rule, etc. If modifications to the theory are nevertheless necessary in film, this is far more true of rock videos which are embedded within the different televisual apparatus.

Partly because this apparatus manifests what Baudrillard has called the new "universe of communication," many videos do not evoke the pre-Oedipal and Oedipal configurations of the classical Hollywood film that belonged in the earlier "intimate" universe. We saw in the last chapter how Baudrillard characterizes this universe as "projective, imaginary and symbolic," as against the world of the "non-reflecting surface, an immanent surface where operations unfold – the smooth operational surface of communication." We will see the implications of this new, post-Oedipal world for the representation of women shortly, when I discuss videos by female stars. But the post-Oedipal world is, of course, manifest in the postmodernist video, and exists in some of the classical type that appear rather to play with Freudian voyeurism and fetishism than to take those gazes seriously.

Interestingly enough, the earlier Oedipal mode is evident in both the romantic and nihilist videos, although it emerges in ways rather different from that in the Hollywood film. I will begin by comparing and contrasting a romantic and nihilist video figuring male stars in order to show the ways in which rock videos take up parts of the Oedipal scenario other than the classical male gaze, and then further contrast these with a postmodernist male video. The second half of the chapter will then be devoted to a detailed analysis of the various kinds of gaze manifest in select videos by female stars. Let me again note that in providing in-depth analyses of individual videos I am rather unnaturally "stopping the 24-hour flow" for the same reasons as in Chapter 4, and with the same risks of assuming more impact than there really can be within that flow to the subject positions analyzed. The whole point about MTV is that the experience is defined by the flow of texts; in its very structure, this embodies Baudrillard's concept of "an optimalization of the play of possibilities" as against texts representing objects "of psychological sanctuary." Nevertheless, if we do "stop the flow," we can find texts that remain from the "old" universe and that do arguably rely on Oedipal processes.

The romantic and nihilist videos, then, as individual texts still work out of the Oedipal scenario. But, significantly, they are structured around aspects of that scenario rarely dealt with in the classical Hollywood film or indeed other major narrative forms that tend to rely on voyeurism and fetishism. Also, interestingly enough, each stresses an aspect of the psychic familial constellation at the opposite extreme from the other. The nihilist, heavy metal video involves adolescent male Oedipal identification with the phallus as signifier. This is a more deliberate and excessive identification than that involved in the voyeuristic gaze, and is more violent than the normal fetishistic one to which it *is* linked. Instead of seeking to find the phallus in the woman, the nihilist video seeks to appropriate the feminine to the phallus through the device of the masquerade.

Let me dwell on this a moment since the use of the masquerade here represents one kind of androgynous address in MTV videos. This form of masquerade, often accompanying the parade of virility (cf. the Brazilian Festival where men routinely dress up as women), seeks to control the feared feminine, the feared difference, by possessing it, incorporating it within the self. A Bakhtinian reading of this might argue that the adoption of female traits and clothing manifests a beneficial carnivalesque gender reversal. But while the carnival process *may* be at work for some stars (Motley Crue), something else is going on in those analyzed here. If I possess the feminine myself, it seems to say, then I no longer need to satisfy the desire for woman *outside* myself, thus avoiding the terror of so doing. Significantly, this is a very different function of the masquerade than that outlined by Mary Ann Doane when, following Lacan, she talks of women "operating a performance of femininity, a masquerade, by means of an accumulation of accessories . . . all designed to mask the absence of a lack."[4] The male masquerade uses a similar adoption of feminine accessories to different ends. That is, here the accessories do not *stand in* for lack (the male has the phallus), as with the female masquerade, but are used in an attempt to deny that there *is* any separate sexual difference that would necessitate accepting the possibility of lack. The strategy renders the feminine non-male rather than Other, as in the parallel strategy of "disguising" woman in masculine dress (viz. the many 1930s and 1940s films involving stars like Dietrich, Hepburn, Russell, and Crawford, which show women stepping into the male public sphere).

The nihilist video thus, seeks to eliminate or to master the mother, displacing desire for her into sadistic possession. The romantic video, by contrast, involves precisely the pre-Oedipal, dyadic and illusory oneness with the mother. Far from annihilating the mother, these videos, as we'll see, inscribe her gaze into their very aesthetic structure as much as the nihilist video inscribes the phallic gaze. The distinction between these gazes corresponds to that between Freud's scopophilic gaze and that of Lacan's mirror phase. While film theory often evokes the screen/mirror analogy in a general way, the differences between the Freudian, Oedipal and phallic gaze – relying on identification with the father, and the pre-Oedipal Lacanian mirror gaze – that involves merging with and separation from the mother, have not been developed. The fact that rock videos incorporate the mutual mother—child gaze at all is significant in revealing a certain opening up within popular culture of a terrain largely absent from the classical Hollywood film.

Let me briefly elaborate the differences between these two gazes within the Lacanian paradigm. As noted in Chapter 3, the mirror gaze represents the transitional phase between the pre-Oedipal and the phallic phases. It represents the start of realizing subjectivity (which is really a *split* subjectivity) as the child at once clings onto the illusory oneness with the mother in the world of the imaginary *and* begins to be aware of the mother as an object distinct from itself. The imaginary unitary self (whether a mother-self Self or a mirror-self Self) is now split into two objects: mother and self; mirror-image and self.

This process is only possible through the child's recourse to the world of the symbolic. Paradoxically, and despite Lacan's notorious scorn for object-relations psychoanalysis, the child's situation at the moment of entry into the symbolic involves an object relation (i.e. the relation to the mother or its image) that is in the process of being replaced by the word/image/representation as the device for enabling subjectivity and separation from the mother to take place.

This is perhaps most clear in the oft-discussed "fort"/"da" game occurring at approximately the same time as the mirror phase and also involved with the constitution of the unconscious.[5] There the mother is clearly replaced by the cotton reel that, as a symbol which replaces her, enables the child to conceptualize her absence and return. The child's subjectivity begins to be constituted, as we saw earlier, through the relation to a *representation* of the Other, just as in the mirror phase, subjectivity is constituted by the gaze of the Other.

The use that Lacan makes of the object relation is naturally different from that of the analysts he opposes, who are concerned with issues of bonding and attachment after the entry into language; for Lacan, the object-relation rather *ends* with the onset of the phallic phase and the entry into the symbolic. The unconscious is formed at this point, as the child enters the sphere of desire (desire being precisely that which cannot be fulfilled). From this point on, everyone in the Oedipal triangle will take his/her position from the phallus as signifier: objects are henceforth what Lacan calls "petit objects à," constituted through language and unavailable otherwise, in contrast to the "real" objects with which people supposedly interact in the object-relations schools.

The romantic and the nihilist video take their respective gazes from these two early childhood phases. The romantic video functions in the pre-symbolic dyadic terrain between the illusory merging with the mother and the phallicism that follows the mirror phase. Also important here is an even earlier pre-Oedipal phase (from birth to about six months) in which (as recent mother—infant interaction studies by Stern and Fraiberg have shown) the gaze at the mother's face provides a pleasure crucial in development.[6] In this phase, the child, still not aware of the mother's face as separate from itself, views it, like other objects, as a continuation of an undifferentiated world.

Many romantic videos manifest an unusual preoccupation with the human face, in constant close-ups and lap-dissolves that suggest regression to the moment when the mother's face represented plenitude, oneness, non-Oedipal pleasure. Since representation cannot but take place within the symbolic realm, we have an attempt to approximate the earlier imaginary and dyadic phase through technical devices that mimic the mutual mother—infant gaze.

Before looking at Paul Young's successful "Every Time You Go Away" as an example of this kind of gaze, let me make a comment about gender as it relates to the pre-symbolic. In pre-dating the construction of sexual identity through the acquisition of sentence structure and the grammatical "he"/"she" identifications, the pre-symbolic phase represents a libidinal, genderless reaching out in all directions. It thus differs markedly from the later phallic phase, which is firmly rooted in socially constructed sex difference identifications. Romantic videos are interesting precisely because of a certain bi-sexuality, which must be distinguished from the androgyny of the nihilist video.

By bi-sexuality, I mean that both genders, whether as performers or as spectators, position themselves (and are positioned) similarly. The basic structure is the mother—infant dyad, and in the pre-symbolic phase the biological sex of the child (the mark that will become defining once the child enters the symbolic) does not matter. Whether male or female, the child experiences merging, illusory oneness with the mother; and while from the mother's position the sex of the child may make a superficial social difference, in terms of the *structure* of her relationship to the child it is not significant.

Romantic videos thus position both the male and the female spectator in what has traditionally been the "feminine" (i.e. passive) position. Whether the performer is male or female, and whether a male or female is being addressed as the lost object, makes little difference. It is the narrative situation of merging, loss, and separation that governs identification rather than the gender-based gaze—image dichotomies of the nihilist and classical types.

Nevertheless, it is significant that recently more male stars have been creating romantic songs with corresponding videos. Earlier, as noted in Chapter 4, the romantic video tended to be the province of female stars like Cyndi Lauper ("Time After Time"), Stevie Nicks ("If Anyone Falls in Love"), Heart ("What About Love"), etc. The male star in such videos, like Lionel Ritchie in "Hello," used to be an exception. But in 1983-4 the type had been virtually taken over by the male star and is often top of the countdown. Besides Phil Collins's "One More Night," Foreigner's "I Want to Know What Love Is," and Paul Young's "Every Time You Go Away," already mentioned as in the top slot for several weeks, there was Bob Dylan's "Tight Connection to My Heart," Simple Minds' "Don't You Forget About Me," Julian Lennon's "Much Too Late," Paul McCartney's "No More Lonely Nights." It is less common to find current female stars singing about loss and separation, although about the time that she was pregnant, Pat Benatar did make a sentimental, romantic video, "We Belong," complete with angelic children in a church-like choir and artificial nature setting. (Eurythmics' 1985 "There Must Be an Angel" video is possibly a parody of the Benatar tape, set, as it is, in some kind of Grecian heaven where children flit around with deliberately artificial-looking wings.)[7]

In focusing on the desire for merging with the loved one and on

96

the lost (mother) object, videos elicit regression to the mirror phase, i.e. to beginning awareness of subjectivity through the need to separate from the mother. At this point, castration and Oedipal rivalry are not issues, there being merely a wish to return to the period of illusory oneness. Significantly, the female figure, as lost object, is rarely set up as voyeuristic object of the male gaze (The Cars' ''Why Can't I have You?'' and the Eurythmics' ''Here Comes the Rain Again'' are rare exceptions to this). She is rather imaged with longing and tenderness (as in Foreigner's ''I Want To Know What Love Is''), or simply not imaged at all, her being merely conjured up by the song words and the hero's longing (as in Collins's ''One More Night'').

Like the infant in the Stern and Fraiberg studies already mentioned, the MTV spectator is silent listener/gazer in a one-way process, relying on the close-ups of the performer's face and on the tone/pitch/ rhythm of the music for stimulation. Unlike the baby, the MTV spectator can decode the verbal information of the lyric, but in practice rarely has time to do so, taken up as she/he is by the movement of the visuals and the flow of the music. What we have is a structure of interaction with the image not unlike that of the baby vis-à-vis the mother's face.

Before going on to demonstrate this more clearly by analyzing Paul Young's ''Every Time You Go Away,'' let me clarify what I am trying to argue here. I am not denying that the male appeal to the lost mother object can be seen as merely a reassertion of the traditional patriarchal essentializing of woman as Ideal Mother; what I am trying to argue is that, given that MTV is working within the patriarchal symbolic, it is interesting to find emphasis on a basically *genderless* yearning for the mother (i.e. that place can now be occupied by *either* sex, whereas in traditional patriarchal conventions it is denied the girl – she is to long for the *father*). A second interesting point is that Young, as protagonist in the video, does *not* remain locked into the child position but is also seen to occupy the nurturing *female* position. It is precisely the multiple identifications in the narrative on the part of both protagonist and diegetic spectators that I find interesting. It is true that the mother is literally relegated to absence, but the video so inscribes her gaze as arguably to make itself more powerfully experienced than in the literal images (as in Lauper's ''Time After Time,'' discussed later on) of other videos.

ROCKING AROUND THE CLOCK

Part of the much touted "British Invasion," Paul Young comes out of 1960s soul music, and his performance style was inspired by studying videos of 1960s soul singers like James Brown. He is quoted in a recent *New York Times* article as being as obsessed with performers as with singers, but not necessarily finding stars who combine both aspects in ways he admires. "Some of the best performers, like Mick Jagger and Adam Ant," he notes, "aren't my favorite vocalists. As a singer I admire Sam Cooke the most of all. His diction is incredible and, although I haven't seen a video, the presence that comes off his records is enough."[8]

The performance aspect of "Every Time You Go Away" betrays Young's enthusiasm for Jagger, at least. Rarely still for a moment, he is seen leaping about the stage, bandying the microphone pole like a lance, or in one shot rolling on the floor toward the outstretched arms of his fans. At one point, he takes off his shirt and sends it flying into the crowd; other close-up shots show him reaching toward the outstretched arms and hands of his fans.

This video represents an extraordinarily sensitive, virtually poetic interweaving of musical sounds, Young's voice, the words of Daryl Hall's ballad and the visual images. The overall effect is of sailing or floating – an effect produced by the device of multiple dissolves and superimpositions as the dominant mode of moving from one image to the next. While there are obviously some straight cuts, dissolves predominate; often the superimposition happens on movement either of the camera itself or of Young on stage. Meanwhile, the musical composition and instrumentation convey the same floating effect in the contrapuntal use of Young's flowing voice rising up against the soft, continuous drums, cymbals, and electric sitar (an instrument that Stephen Holden notes has been little used since the late 1960s).[9] The instrumentation is sufficiently complex and unusual to carry the repetition of the main theme lines, "Every time you go away/ You take a little piece of me with you," which always come as a relief after the preceding build up to "Can't you see/ We got everything," at which time the drums and cymbals get louder and more insistent, receding then down to the quieter, melodious tune of "Every time. . . ."

The visuals basically consist of intercutting between two sets of footage: there is footage from one or more live performances intercut with an abstract studio set, consisting of a floor with wavy lines

98

"Joy": taken from a mother—infant interaction study, this image shows the baby's ecstatic response to its mother's presence. Images from Young's video (easily identified) mimic this look but we were refused permission to reprint them.

"Loss": taken from the same study, this image shows the baby expressing loss and anxiety at its mother's absence. Images from the Young video show a forlorn longing close to this look, but again we were refused permission to reprint them here.

on it, either to represent water or the lines on a section of an old tree trunk (but nature anyway). Young stands on this set, sometimes half enmeshed in a fishing net (the sea idea again), with fishing lamps behind him; sometimes his face in close-up is covered by water-like lines or we see these lines in back of the frame, creating a misty, tearful effect.

The stage shots focus heavily on Young's interaction with his fans. In an early shot, repeated later on, Young receives flowers from a fan; rarely is there a shot of him on stage that does not include the fans' arms in front or rear of the frame, or show them packed into the huge auditorium. He is tender and responsive to them, the image usually showing his back bending over the fans in a nurturing, loving fashion, leaning toward them and stretching out his hands. Occasionally we have close-ups of the fans' faces, when we are able to see their rapt, adoring expression; their gaze is fixed unwaveringly on him and on his every movement and their arms reach out to touch him in response to his gesture. In one shot, Young literally runs across the wide stage and rolls down on the floor among the delirious, caressing fans.

These images seem to evoke being held in loving embrace, being nurtured and cared for, as the mother cares for her infant. The fans love Young and he in turn loves them, and the video shows ecstatic expressions on everyone's part during their interaction. Meanwhile, the images intercut from the studio set focus more on loss and separation – on, that is, the mother's absence. Here the often extreme close-ups of Young's face show a forlorn, lost look such as the infant might have on discovering the mother's departure. The contrast between fulfillment and loss is stressed by the cutting: for instance, after an exuberant image of Young rolling on the floor with the fans (no words on the track), we cut to an extreme close-up of Young's forlorn face as, with eyes closed, he lip-synches the lines "Go on and go free/Baby you're too close to see" into the microphone (watery-lines in back of the image suggest tears). Another similar contrast takes place a little earlier in the video, where we go from an image of Young with his rapt fans, and another of him bending over the fans, to a shot of him in the studio set, caught behind the fishing net as he sings the lines "You take a piece of me with you."

Later on, the exuberance of a simulated plenitude with his fans on stage is intercut in rapid succession with the net image (obviously signifying emotional entrapment). These net shots are usually taken from a high angle, suggesting the hero's smallness and vulnerability, while the stage shots show him often in the foreground, looming large against the fans.

Towards the end of the video, we get a delirious, merged kind of sensation deliberately created through the play with the image. Young is on stage, when suddenly the image begins to turn around, dissolving to a bird's eye view of him on the studio set, still turning around, while a larger image of him appears on the right of the frame. This dissolves to a fast-moving camera sailing up to Young's figure in wide-angle in the center of the set, then to a very high angle of him small in frame, and onto his face in close-up superimposed on him performing as he sings "You think I don't care/ But baby I'm with you everywhere." This leads into the final moments of the video in which we see images of Young reaching out to his fans, of the three-man chorus at the rear of the stage (who have been imaged from time to time, gesturing the "Me"/"You" positions in the song line "You take a piece of me with you"), the whole ending with a close-up of Young's face immersed in the watery-lines as his voice sails above the chorus singing the lyric against the instruments.

The total effect of this video is to leave the spectator with a pleasurable mixture of loss and fulfillment. Whether male or female, we identify with Young and his desire to merge with the lost mother object; we have vicarious gratification in the images of Young with his fans, when the ecstasy of momentary merging spills over to the viewer through the technical devices mentioned. Both the infant girl and boy long equally to merge with the mother, so that Young's being male does not prevent female identification with his urge. In fact, in the stage shots, he takes on the symbolic role of the mother, interchanging this with his role as the abandoned child in the studio images. The viewer thus plays out both positions along with the protagonist, getting a series of vicarious gratifications through so doing.

In contrast to this largely pre-Oedipal gaze in the romantic video, the nihilist type relies on the aggressive phallic gaze already referred to. This does not necessarily mean, however, that the address is exclusively to the heterosexual male, as it basically is in the classical category that derives from the voyeuristic gaze of the Hollywood film. A very complicated set of discourses structures the nihilist, heavy metal video, and the address is therefore also complicated – including homo-eroticism and female masochism in its appeal. Whereas the romantic video is structured around humanist notions of bonding and attachment, the nihilist one, in accord with its originally rebellious if often nihilist stance, deplores humanist solutions and speaks violence and destruction without compunction.

This address to violence appeals largely to young males, as is particularly evident in live performances and other shows involving live audiences. (At a recent heavy metal laser show in New York, for instance, the audience consisted almost entirely of groups of young men together. The few women there were safely in the company of two or more men. Deborah Frost in a recent *Village Voice* article did, however, note that more and more women were to be seen at heavy metal live performance shows, suggesting a shifting trend.[10]) But the androgynous aspects of the address, most evident in the performance video, complicate things. The address creates an energetic erotic appeal that is often violent and sadistic, and that consists in a split between a "feminized" outward appearance and "masculine" aggressive behavior. Significantly, most androgynous singers of this type are male (e.g. Duran Duran, Billy Idol, Motley Crue). Eurythmics' Annie Lennox is an exception, but even she belongs in a second, softer androgynous group in which I would put David Bowie, Michael Jackson, and Boy George. These are not so concerned to stress the masculine that lies beneath the feminized veneer, and are less obviously erotic.

In the main type of nihilist video that retains the stage setting, and often figures heavy metal or new wave groups, the male body is deliberately set up as object of desire: zoom shots pick up male crotches and bare chests in an erotic manner and instruments are presented as unabashed phallic props. The camera focuses aggressively on the performers' bodies as they stand front-stage, fans' arms stretching out toward them, often cutting in and isolating, deliberately garishly (effects made more strident by wide-angle lenses), crotches, buttocks, widespread legs. There are some facial close-ups and the performers still provide a centering focus for the incoherent images, but instead of evoking the gentle, mutual mother–infant

102

interaction of the romantic video, these videos rather adopt a challenging, aggressive stance toward the fans and spectators. The camera focuses on the sexual/genital areas – the body rather than the face – and on the often outlandish, extraordinary costumes of the stars and band members. The camera often sways with the male bodies, and figures are filmed in slow motion, often jumping in the air, spread-eagled, as in Van Halen's "Jump." The aim is clearly to shock and to violate accepted social norms.

The female form is often simply absent from this type of nihilist video but, if present, she is usually also dressed in tight leather dress, high heels, sporting long, spiked hair. The iconography, like that of the males, suggests bondage and sadistic sexuality. Let me demonstrate some of these characteristics by looking at two nihilist style videos of rather different casts.

First, Billy Idol's "Rebel Yell," which was near the top of the MTV Countdown in Fall 1984. Very much in the tradition of American, as against British punk, Idol has fostered an image of snarling meanness, not unlike that of Sid Vicious of the British Sex Pistols but without Vicious's political base.[11] Idol's main stance is that of an angry, formless rebelliousness; his main aim, Nietzschean style, is to transvalue dominant ideology and to shock the bourgeoisie. Instead of kindness and helpfulness, he fosters hate, motiveless rage; instead of nurturing, he represents attack and hurt.

On first viewing, "Rebel Yell" appears to be one long, continuous scream; visuals, the musical sounds and rhythms, the song-words and Idol's use of his body, all conspire to construct an embattled spectator, on the receiving end of a boxing glove. The video remains for its entire length within the confines of the stage on which it is set, and the mise-en-scène is very deliberately designed to evoke the black, angry tone of the song. There is a heavy reliance on lighting devices familiar from German Expressionism and film noir; for instance, the spot-lights create pyramid-shaped panels of light, keeping to a blue and red color scheme, that are shed over the individual performers, isolating them in their own color-bound sphere. The stage is basically lurid and shrouded in smokiness much of the time. Its edges cannot therefore be seen so that one has the sense of an endless, timeless space that is No Place. In this murky space, the band members are variously highlighted as noted, but the lighting of

103

course favors Idol. Usually, it is back-lighting, familiar from German Expressionism, that illuminates his short, punk-style blonde hair standing straight up. The lead guitarist, dressed in deliberate contrast to Idol in long leather jacket and pants, and sporting longer black hair, is often lit with a triangular slice of blue or red light that frames him behind Idol, the smoky swirls in the light providing a surreal effect. When we cut, twice, to the female pianist, scantily dressed in red, her blonde hair is also back-lit, giving a similar eerie effect. There are few long shots of the stage from the fans' point of view, as was common in the Young video, no corresponding long shots of the auditorium containing the fans either, and no studio shots away from the stage to provide an extended narrative context. Rather, the camera remains glued to Idol's face and body, or to those of his lead guitarist, with infrequent shots of the other band members or of the fans' faces at the edge of the stage. Often, the frame shows a rear shot of the fans' black-gloved hands and shadowed arms, mimicking Idol's angry fist/arm gesture, with Idol's figure facing the camera in medium close-up.

The result of this close-in camera is claustrophobic: the spectator simply cannot get away from the anger that is being directed often specifically at him/her. For instance, in one section, when Idol is not singing, the drums beat out a regular series of notes, and Idol punches directly at the camera with his lethal-looking, spiked, leather gloves and wide wrist band. He wields this "weapon" throughout, but usually directs it in medium shot at the fans, attacking and battling with them.

The claustrophobic effect is mitigated somewhat by the shifts in the mood and the rhythm that follow the phases of the song's moods. While these are within a narrow range, the changes do provide the spectator with a breathing space (and presumably permit Idol's own vocal chords a slight rest!). The video opens energetically and loudly with Idol screaming in his husky, throaty voice the main theme-lines of the song, oft-repeated: "In the midnight hour/ She cried more, more, more/ With a rebel yell/ She cried more, more, more." This is repeated several times, while the camera cuts between close-ups of Idol's face and spiked, gloved hand grasping the mike, and medium close-ups of his guitarists on either side of him. Idol here points his finger directly at the camera, punctuating

104

his deliberately articulated "More, more, more" with stabs at the viewer and the fans, his body meanwhile also moving up and down in time with the heavy, steady bang of drums and guitars. The shots of the lead guitarist focus on his guitar as a phallic prop, his side-angled body shot at crotch-level emphasizing the phallicism.

A quieter moment emerges with the words "She once said I'm bad/She's mean, she's bad," and the camera now closes in on Idol's face in wide-angle lens, as if for a confession. The tone remains quieter as he goes on to express his disgust at the woman's leaving, with "What set you free/I brought you to be with me, babe," rising in volume as he angrily screams his need: "I need you here by me/ Because [loudest now] in the midnight hour/She cried more, more, more/With a rebel yell/More, more, more."

This is followed by focus on the lead guitarist in front frame, very close-in to the fans, letting his guitar scream and whine as he brandishes it like a sword/phallus. Idol meanwhile is now positioned in rear of the frame, so that his muscular, bare-chested body with leather jacket open, legs astride in their leather pants and boots, is deliberately silhouetted. The guitarist then stops, Idol comes to front frame, and with snarls and grimaces he punches at the camera, timing his punches to the loud, steady drum beat. The drummer's image is intercut with Idol's a few times, and then with the guitarist when he enters the musical stream again.

The rhythm then slows, and Idol, at his most vulnerable in the entire video, sidles head down along the front row of fans and admits "I'd walk the wall with you babe/Then thousand miles with you babe/I'd dry your tears, babe/A million times for you, you, you/I'd sell my soul, soul, soul/For money to burn/For you, you, you." Here Idol acts more gently toward the fans, looking down at them, still pointing but less aggressively. The shot is longer than previous ones, the intercutting now ceasing temporarily.

But gradually, he works up to his anger again, screaming "I'd give you all because/In the midnight hour . . . " and so on, repeatedly, until the video ends on the same, loud, angry note with which started. The intercutting between Idol and his guitarists resumes, and the camera angles move lower even than before, highlighting the crotches of both Idol and the guitarist as they stand astride in front of the now wildly waving and moving fans.

This video, like other similar nihilist ones of its type, manifests the opposite psychic familial constellation to the romantic one by Paul Young. Instead of mimicking the mother—infant interaction as the moment of loss and separation, "Rebel Yell" voices the sadistic desire to master and possess the mother, to hear her cry "More, more, more." The hero will do anything for her if only she will succumb to him and worship his phallus as much as he does himself.

Iconographically, the video sets up Idol and his friends as signifiers for the phallus. Idol's carefully chosen name reinforces his self-fetishization; he takes his own body as a representation of what he wants to have, namely the phallus. And to *have* the phallus, it is necessary for the woman to *be* the phallus for him – hence the hero's need of her.

The self-conscious androgyny of a nihilist video like this one by Billy Idol, where we have images similar to those increasingly adopted by adult popular culture and by fashion and advertising, has far different sources and implications than the non-Oedipal, genderless gaze of the romantic video. There is an attempt to construct sexuality as undifferentiated, in opposition to the Hollywood construction of sexuality so as to emphasize difference; but while the new construction seems to attempt a transcendence of sex difference, does it really accomplish this?

One could rather argue that a video like "Rebel Yell" actually addresses both male and female desires as constructed within patriarchy – namely the male sadistic desire, the corresponding female masochistic one. In this reading, the female fans predominating in Idol's video signify female identification with the object of Idol's sadism, desiring to be desired, desiring also perhaps to be mastered. (It is significant that while the object of the protagonist's rage within the diegesis is not imaged, her "double" *is* represented in the bodies of the female fans that Idol addresses extra-diegetically.)

While the ambiguity in the sexual address in a nihilist video like this one typifies postmodernism, it seems likely that the androgynous address of many heavy metal videos reflects a restructuring of sexual difference so as to appropriate the feminine rather than a totally new sexual paradigm. However, it is possible that such restructurings are preparing for a new paradigm.

The hated female object *is* imaged in Idol's recent "White Wedding," where the nihilism structures the entire narrative, and where the address seems unambiguously male. A desecration of the whole concept of "holy matrimony," the video turns marriage into an expressionist-style horror-show – a gothic funeral rather than an idyllic romantic ritual. Many of the assorted onlookers are dressed in black leather outfits, with chains, while the bridesmaid wears a black funereal veil. The bride's middle-class-looking parents are ridiculous in the "church" setting that looks like something out of Lang's *Metropolis*. The climax to the ceremony comes when Idol grabs the bride's hand, and, as he sings "It's a nice day to start again," rips the bride's finger with his barbed-wire ring. After a series of close-ups of the bride's screaming face, in slow motion, the assembly salutes the couple, Nazi-style. Bourgeois codes are symbolically finally violated as Idol smashes through a stained-glass window in a rain of glass shards. The bride is contrasted with three sinister looking blonde women in shiny black leather suits who dance behind Idol as they appropriate the "altar" after the bride has gone. The nihilist "message" is spelled out in the final scene, which has the bride dancing headily in a typical bourgeois kitchen, as all the normal household accoutrements explode; Idol, leering into the frame (in wide-angle lens), meanwhile sings, "There is nothing safe in this world/There is nothing pure in this world/There is nothing sure in this world/There is nothing left in this world." As if to underscore the point, the last image shows the "bride" (is she now a corpse?) covered in her white veil, like a mannequin, while Idol and his three black-leathered women dance in the front of the frame.

The second nihilist video that I'll discuss, Scorpion's "Rock You Like a Hurricane," also includes female representations and has a rather different sexual address. Made by a West German group, "Rock You Like a Hurricane" has a more complex heavy metal score than that in Idol's video. Consisting likewise of a large drum/cymbal unit and electric guitars, the instrumentation is more creative and imaginative and the voice is used contrapuntally in interesting ways. While loud and unmelodious in the manner of heavy metal, "Rock You" nevertheless manages not to overwhelm with relatively meaningless screaming sounds as in the Idol video. There is actually an inventive musical interlude half-way through the video where the instruments take over as against merely accompanying the voice as they do much of the time.

107

ROCKING AROUND THE CLOCK

In contrast to the two previous videos, there is a dramatic narrative situation here but it still permits the performance element to remain. Paradoxically, the precise narrative situation (which is anyway unclear) is less important than the interconnection between sounds and visuals. Both music and visuals take off from the idea of a hurricane and the resulting "rocking" (the whole perhaps a pun on rock music itself); the musical score mimics storm sounds, and the line of the music sweeps up and down like wind roaring. Meanwhile, the camera work duplicates the notion of "rocking" already present, consisting of very rapid cutting of single shots (sometimes almost too fast to capture in still frame), of extremely low and wide angle shots, and of sweeping movements around and along the bars of the cage in which the performers are trapped. The shots are mainly close-ups of the bodies of the performers and, sometimes, the women, creating a claustrophobic effect similar to that in Idol's video; but here there are a few extreme long shots, showing a high-angle view down on the entire cage, the women ranged around, and the white leaders (or whatever) in the rear.

The mise-en-scène is rather similar to that in the Idol video although, as noted, it does have a narrative dimension. The men are in some alien, science fiction otherwhere; they seem to be trapped first in long tubes and then (within the tubes? it is not clear) inside a cage. This cage "rocks," its walls moving in and out under the pressure of hordes of women locked outside the cage and evidently trying to reach the men within. The performers (especially the guitarists and the star singer) also rock their own bodies while they play or sing, so that at times the entire image is on the move. The atmosphere is murky, hazy, and generally unclear. There is a similar expressionist/noir mood to everything, here mixed with a sense of outerspace or of some other planet.

I am particularly interested in the representation of the women in this video since the situation is clearly an Oedipal one. To begin with, the men are subject to the Law of the Father, represented by the sinister, white-robed men, without proper faces, who stand around an alarming fire for which the men may be destined. On one level, there is a battle for power going on between the captives and these rulers.

But second, the men are evidently being seduced by the women in the community, whose situation vis-à-vis the rulers is unclear. The first woman we see, in close-up and attempting to seduce the hero, is dressed in skimpy sequined clothes (is she the Queen, wife of a ruler?) and has a mask over her eyes. But all the rest of the women are far more poorly dressed, although their eyes are still covered now by black make-up that looks like a blindfold. They have on primitive tops and mini-skirts and wear long black gloves which appear like snakes reaching through the bars to grasp the men.

The men seem to be in an impossible Oedipal situation, caught between the seductive mother and the castrating father. The women catch one of the guitarists through the bars and maul his head about before letting him go. In another shot towards the end, we see one of the women breaking through the bars of the cage and looming up, slow motion, toward the hero. The women are associated with fearsome imagery, since in the following shot we see them walk toward the camera up some mist-laden, tree-lined path, passing as they do so the agonized faces of men, crossed by thorns and sticks, who are bound in the woods. Finally, as the video ends, the men appear to have freed themselves, although they only have the same horrifying path to run along.

In contrast to the Idol video, this one embodies a more classical Oedipal scenario showing fear of the seductive mother. But interestingly, the mother is blinded, unable to see, and the fathers do not seem to have normal eyes either. The heroes thus emerge as both the ones who can see and who are virile despite their captivity. Shots again focus on the male crotches and guitarists use their instruments as phallic props as in the Idol video. Somehow, the heroes transcend their potentially passive "captive" situation through their sheer energy and inherent virility, evidently escaping the death that seemed to await them.

Even more than the Idol video, "Rock You" seems to close out any possible position for the female spectator other than identifying with woman as sign for something in the male unconscious. The male spectator may vicariously enjoy the representation of desiring women, but the female desire is merely symbolic. The women are more like automatons than living flesh, their gestures mechanical, perhaps ordered. They seem to lack any desire of their own, despite their narrative situation as trying to get into the cage. Once again, although via very different means, the video establishes an explicitly phallic gaze deriving from the Oedipal rather than the pre-Oedipal phase.

The second type of Oedipal gaze, that is the explicitly voyeuristic one, I have relegated to a separate category, the classical. This type lacks many of the qualities of the nihilist video, such as the blurring of genres, the sense of an alien, unstable world, the nihilism and androgynous address, etc. The type stays closer to the narrative style of the classical Hollywood film, although most do not adhere to classical cutting codes, eye-line matches, 30 degree rule and so on. In addition, the self-consciousness about what is being shown does position the videos in a different relation to the voyeuristic gaze.

Good examples of this type are Rod Stewart's "Infatuation" or the more recent John Parr's "Naughty Naughty." The first is "classical" in the sense of setting up a typical narrative situation of a young man spying on the beautiful faithless femme fatale being pursued by an older man, probably a gangster. Where the video differs from film noir is in its deliberate foregrounding of the hero's voyeurism by having him set up his camera in front of the window where the woman undresses. We have shots of him photographing her through the slots in the blind, the frame including both his body (front frame) and hers across the way, moving seductively to the music. We get close-up stills of the photos taken, and in one shot the hero dances in front of a huge blow-up of the woman in her skimpy bikini. Obsessed with her, he follows her around, constantly spying upon her through doors, windows, and from balconies.

A silent, distant figure, often in swimsuit and dark glasses, the woman merely stands in for something in the male unconscious, reflecting the theories that feminist film critics have developed in relation to the Hollywood film. Nevertheless, as noted there is a new self-consciousness about these voyeuristic videos that positions them differently from the unselfconscious classical Hollywood film. Stewart's words and gestures suggest rather a bored "déjà vu" than real anger that the woman is faithless and takes new lovers. "Oh, no, not again/It hurts so good, I don't understand," he says, repeatedly. There is a comic juxtaposition of the hero with his cat gazing into, and desiring, the goldfish in the bowl, suggesting an

110

identification between the hero's and the cat's gaze. The video is lively, semi-comic and music and visuals keep up a fast, pleasing rhythm.

Parr's "Naughty Naughty" is in many ways more obnoxious because of the hero's arrogant, sneering attitude both in general and specifically in relation to women. The only thing that slightly lessens the video's strident sexism is, again, its apparent self-consciousness about the issues it treats. It opens with an arrogant hero giving up his job working on fancy cars because the boss catches him fondling the car enviously. The hero screeches out of the garage in his sports car, soon picking up a girl, whom he eyes possessively and then tries to seduce. Refusing to "be a girl like that" she jumps out of the car, throwing her necklace after it. The video next shows the hero happily in the midst of a cluster of sexy girls, all hungrily devouring his body. After this, he is once again on the road. The first girl has now evidently regretted her rejection of the hero, and allows herself to be picked up once again.

The video ends with them sailing off together in the car, the hero having his cake and eating it too! A far more deliberate and humorous parody of objectifying the female body is David Lee Roth's successful "California Girls." While I appreciate the parody of seaside postcard humor in this video, and the fact that it mocks tourists as much as anything else, the way the female body is (ab)used is disturbing. The video is built on the concept of voyeurism, which it laughs at without critiquing. The female bodies are set up as silent, statuesque entities for the camera and the tour guide to handle and gaze at without compunction.

Robert Palmer's "Addicted to Love" has a similar set of impassive female bodies, this time clothed like identical store-window mannequins in tight black mini-dresses: They surround Palmer as his musical accompanists and the camera freely plays with their eyes, heavily lipsticked mouths, and nude legs, rendering them passive objects of desire. The same is true of Palmer's recent "I Didn't Mean to Turn You On," which has this time *two* sets of women dressed identically, with whose sexy bodies the camera likewise plays, while the hero in the center has them all to himself!

The line of impassive female forms recalls a similar parade of the female body in the Romantics' "Talking in Your Sleep," where the

111

hero walks through the lines of sleeping women who stand passively in their various, often sexy, nightdresses, and caresses their bodies with his flashlight, and sometimes with his lips. He is celebrating the fact that he has access to his lover's unconscious since she cannot keep her secrets from him because she talks in her sleep. We have here the ultimate voyeuristic fantasy of total male (in)sight into the female, with the resulting control and possession. "You tell me that you want me/You tell me that you need me/You tell me that you love me," he sings. A little later, he notes that "Don't you know you're sleeping/In a spot light" and the visuals show the hero scanning the woman's legs with his torch, revealing black stockings, suspenders, and the classic porn-style corset. This is immediately followed by a shot of the hero putting the finishing touches to the make-up on a large Marilyn Monroe poster, the image responding with seductive lip movements. The idea evidently is that the woman is to be a seductive little girl type, like Monroe. And indeed, many of the sleeping, passive figures are holding teddy bears!

The imagery here clearly looks back, somewhat nostalgically, to the 1950s, perhaps in an unconscious wish to return woman to that (mythical) passive position; a recent video by the Fabulous Thunderbirds, "Tuff Enuff," on the other hand, rather attempts to recuperate the image of the tough new "working woman" that is interestingly combined with the even more recent athletic female look. The deliberately spare, schematic set (it has a vaguely futurist look) suggests both a jungle-gym and a construction site; and indeed, the women who soon appear are dressed so as to connote both construction-site workers (they have on hard-hats) and women working out in the gym (sneakers, sweat-shirts, and shorts). But it turns out that the choreography intends to co-opt both suggestions, and return the women to the place (and status) of sex-objects. The women's movements, that is, increasingly move from those appropriate to construction work to those of the aerobics class, to those of the erotic dancer or the stripper. The band members arrive at the site on their phallic motorbikes and proceed to respond to the women's seductive movements. The climax (sexual, narrative) is achieved when the protagonist discovers the really erotic heroine, who explicitly merges the traditional erotic female with the new tough look as she swaggers in

112

John Cougar Mellencamp, "Hurts So Good"

Cougar Mellencamp's video plays with the recent interest in sado-masochistic imagery.

The play with voyeurism is evident in having the men face the camera and turn away from th women on stage in rear frame.

113

wearing high heels, fancy shorts, and a low-cut blouse, parading long, curly hair.

The choreography situates the originally distinct types of female bodies and movements along a similar signifying chain; women's bodies are made to signify sexuality no matter in what context they are being used. The video manages in this way to trivialize, or even negate, women's newly won efforts for entrance into traditionally masculine work spheres and their equally new interest in hitherto "male" athletics.

A less patronizing, more playful treatment of the female body, in a different mode, is John Cougar Mellencamp's recent "Hurts So Good." This video addresses recent interest in sado-masochism on the part of both young men and women; it is set in some kind of club, where a gang of macho-style motorbike men are gathered to watch two dancing women, dressed (classic porn style) in black skin-tight leotards, fishnet stockings, high-heeled shoes, and covered in chains and neck chokers. In a sense it is all rather harmless and unerotic. The video even plays with the classical voyeurism it first seems to endorse, since in one shot the men face the camera, looking *away from* the women dancing on the stage. But the video symbolizes the open address to sado-masochistic fantasies with women in the "victim" position.

A similar play with sado-masochistic imagery is evident in Prince's "1999." The futurist suggestion is ironic in that the imagery in fact looks back to Nazi sexual iconography, especially in the cutaways from Prince, in his long black leather coat reminiscent of Nazism, to two blonde young women accompanists in short leather outfits and black military caps. Prince's aggressive, phallic stance is more show than meant seriously, however, and again the video manifests a kind of postmodernist play with this well-worn iconography, confusing the spectator as to an appropriate response.

In these more brutal videos, it seems that the sadistic component has taken precedence over the merely voyeuristic and fetishistic one of most videos in this category. While sadism is obviously involved in the latter drives, it is content to express itself through the gaze. Sadism proper, on the other hand, demands release on an object – it

114

demands action. No longer prepared to work through the relationship to the mother via castration anxiety released in abusive visual objectification, it now seeks rather to displace the feared violence to the phallus onto fantasies of violence perpetrated on the female form. This prevalence of sexually violent and graphic material on videos has recently caught the public attention (cf. article by Kandy Stroud in *Newsweek,* May 6 1985), and the Parents' Music Resources Center (PMRC) are presently demanding that warnings be printed on records and cassettes with sexually explicit lyrics and images. (A recent ad by such a group ironically focused not on one of these sexist, sadistic videos by male stars but on Madonna's (possibly ironic but at any rate postmodernist) "Like a Virgin." The ad shows a little girl playing with a doll on a bed and humming "Just like a vi-i-i-r-gin." The voice then offers a warning about such songs.) I am not sure that censorship is desirable, viable or necessary, [12] particularly in the light of the self-parody of many of the videos objected to, but the fact that young teenagers who may not grasp the parody aspects are getting their first conception of an adult female identity through such videos is of concern.

Let me now turn to the representation of the female body and the gender address in videos figuring female stars. First, a word about the frequency of such videos and their cycling across the 24-hour flow, since these aspects are important for understanding the dominating kind of gender address on MTV. Both issues are further linked to the over-arching commercial framework of MTV in that only those female representations considered the most marketable are frequently cycled: and what is most marketable is obviously connected to dominant ideology, to the social imaginary discussed in Chapter 4 and to the organization of the symbolic order around the phallus as signifier.

According to a recent quantifying study of MTV, videos featuring white males take up 83 per cent of the 24-hour flow.[13] Only 11 per cent of MTV videos have central figures who are female (incidentally, the figure is even lower for blacks), and women are typically, like blacks, rarely important enough to be part of the foreground. Brown and Campbell assert that "white women are often shown in passive and solitary activity or are shown trying to gain the attention of a man who ignores them" (p. 104). Among those 11 per

115

cent, the number of videos by women that *are* frequently cycled fall into the first type mentioned, namely those where the position is ambiguous, where what we might call a postmodern feminist stance is evident.

I will discuss what I mean by this "postmodern feminist" stance in a moment, but I want first to note the other kinds of female representations that do appear on the channel, if only rarely, and that I will by analyzing. There are, first, videos in the "socially conscious" category that make the kind of statement one could call "feminist" (e.g. Pat Benatar's "Love is a Battlefield" or her more recent "Sex As a Weapon," or Donna Summer's "She Works Hard for the Money"); these have quite conventional narratives, although they do not adhere strictly to Hollywood codes. Second, there are occasional videos that appear to comment upon the objectifying male gaze (as does arguably Tina Turner's "Private Dancer"), or that deconstruct an established American icon, as in Julie Brown's "The Homecoming Queen's Got a Gun." In these cases the visual strategies creatively embody the deconstructive aims. And finally, some videos attempt to set up a different gaze altogether, or to address some (possible) female gaze, as arguably happens in the recent Aretha Franklin/Annie Lennox "Sisters Are Doin' It For Themselves." Except for Benatar's "Love is a Battlefield," these videos only remained in circulation for a short period of time and then not at a high density rate.

It is important that the channel's format of short, four-minute texts does permit gaps through which a variety of enunciative positions are made available. I am then able to "stop the flow," as it were, in order to concentrate on constructions of the female body other than the prevailing "postmodern feminist" or various "male gaze" constructions. But this is with full awareness that these isolated moments in fact are overridden by the plethora of texts presenting other positions. The various possibilities for "seeing otherwise" in these different figurations of the female body are worth exploring as part of understanding what popular culture *can* do; but the ordinary MTV spectator will in fact get little opportunity for this kind of "seeing." For such female images do not fit into the prevailing desire for the rich sensation of glossy surfaces, bright colours, rapid action, or for the parade of bodies in contemporary clothing that the dominant videos offer.

Let me begin with a video, "Material Girl," featuring Madonna,

116

the female star who perhaps more than any other embodies the new postmodern feminist heroine in her odd combination of seductiveness and a gutsy sort of independence.

"Material Girl" is particularly useful for discussion because it exemplifies a common rock-video phenomenon, namely that of establishing a unique kind of intertextual relationship with a specific Hollywood movie. Because of this, as well as the difficulty of ensuring the text's stance toward what it shows and the blurring of many conventional boundaries, I would put the video in the "postmodern" category in Table 3 (p. 55), despite its containing more narrative than is usual for the type.

As is well-known, "Material Girl" takes off from the famous Marilyn Monroe dance/song sequence in *Gentlemen Prefer Blondes*, namely "Diamonds Are a Girl's Best Friend." The sequence occurs towards the end of the film where Esmond's father has severed Lorelei (Monroe) financially from Esmond, forcing her to earn her living by performing. In this sequence, having finally found her, Esmond is sitting in the audience watching the show. We thus have the familiar

Tommy Noonan as Esmond in *Gentlemen Prefer Blondes*

Esmond's astonished gaze at Monroe from his theatre seat.

117

Marilyn Monroe as Lorelei in *Gentlemen Prefer Blondes*

Monroe surrounded by male suitors as she performs "Diamonds are a Girl's Best Friend."

Hollywood situation, where the woman's performing permits her double articulation as spectacle for the male gaze (i.e. she is object of desire for both the male spectator in the diegetic audience and for the spectator in the cinema watching the film). The strategy formalizes the mirror-phase situation by framing the female body both within the stage proscenium arch and the cinema screen.

During this sequence, which starts with Esmond's astonished gaze at Lorelei from the theater seat (presumably he is surprised anew by Lorelei's sexiness), Lorelei directs her gaze toward the camera that is situated in Esmond's place. The space relations are thus quite simple, there being merely the two spaces of the stage and of the theater audience. We know that the film is being made under the authorial label "Hawkes," that within the diegesis, Monroe and Russell are setting up the action, but that, despite this, the patriarchal world in which they move constrains them and makes only certain avenues available.

When we turn to the video inspired by the Monroe dance sequence, we see that the situation is far more complicated. First, it is unclear who is speaking this video, even on the remote "authorial label" level, since credits are never given in the usual run of things. Is it perhaps Madonna, as historical star subject? Is it "Madonna I," the movie-star protagonist within the "framing" diegesis? Is it "Madonna II," the figure within the musical dance diegesis? Is it the director who has fallen in love with her image and desires to possess her? If we focus first on the visual strategies and then on the soundtrack, you will see that we get different and still confusing answers to the question.

Visually, the director's (D) gaze seems to structure some of the shots, but this is not consistent, as it is in the Monroe sequence. And shots possibly structured by him (or in which he is later discovered to have been present) only occur at irregular intervals. The video begins by foregrounding (perhaps pastiching?) the classical Hollywood male gaze: there is a close-up of the director, played by Keith Carradine (the video thus bows again to the classical film), whom we soon realize is watching rushes of a film starring "Madonna I" with an obsessed, glazed look on his face. "I want her, George," he says; George promises to deliver, as we cut to a two-shot of the men, behind whom we see the cinema screen and Madonna I's image but as yet

ROCKING AROUND THE CLOCK

Madonna, "Material Girl"

A male desire, given birth through the cinematic apparatus.

hear no sound from the performance. The camera closes in on her face, and on her seductive look first out to the camera then sideways to the men around her. As the camera now moves into the screen, blurring the boundaries between screening room, screen, and the film set (the space of the performance that involves the story of the Material Girl, Madonna II), the "rehearsal" (if that is what it was) ends, and a rich lover comes onto the set with a large present for Madonna I.

This then is a desire for the woman given birth through the cinematic apparatus, in classic manner; yet while the sequence seems to *foreground* those mechanisms, it does not appear to critique or in any way comment upon them. In Jameson's terms, this makes the process pastiche rather than parody and puts it in the postmodernist mode. The blurring of the diegetic spaces further suggests postmodernism, as does the following confusion of enunciative stances, taking the visual track alone. For while the D's gaze clearly constructed the first shot-series, it is not clear that his gaze structures the shot where Madonna I receives the present. We still hear the

120

GENDER ADDRESS AND THE GAZE

Madonna, "Material Girl"

Madonna gazes at the camera, intent upon seducing the TV spectator.

whirring sound of a projector, as if this were still the screening room space; and yet we are *inside* that screen – we no longer see the space around the frame, thus disorienting the viewer.

We cut to a close-up of a white phone ringing and a hand picking it up, and are again confused spatially. Where are we? Whose look is this? There has been no narrative preparation for the new space or for the spectator address: the phone monologue by Madonna I (the only time in the entire video that she speaks) establishes the space as her dressing room. As she speaks, the camera behaves oddly (at least in standard Hollywood conventions), dollying back slowly to the door of her room, to reveal standing there the D. Was it then his gaze that structured the shot? At the moment of reaching him, the gaze certainly *becomes* his, Madonna I seen to be its object. The phone monologue that he overhears, along with the viewer, establishes that Madonna I has just received a diamond necklace, which causes the D to throw his present into the waste basket that the janitor happens to be carrying out that moment. It also establishes that Madonna I is *not* the "material girl" of her stage role, since she offers the necklace to her (presumed) girlfriend on the phone.

We now cut back to the stage space that we presume is the film set; it is not clear, since the diegesis does not foreground the filming processes, and yet there is no audience space. Rather, Madonna II sets up a direct rapport with the camera filming the rock video, and therefore with the TV spectator, deliberately playing for him/her rather than for the men in frame. But the spatial disorientation continues: there is a sudden cut to the rear of a flashy red car driving into the studio, followed by shots of Madonna I's elegant body in matching red dress (knees carefully visible), of her rich lover bending over her, and of her face and apparently dismissive reply. Whose gaze is this? Who is enunciating here? As Madonna I leaves the car, we discover the D again, but the series of shots could not have been structured by his gaze.

We cut back to the stage/film set for the most extended sequence of the performance in the video. This sequence follows the Monroe "Diamonds" dance closely, and stands in the strange intertextual relationship already mentioned: we cannot tell whether or not the Monroe sequence is being commented upon, simply used, or ridiculed by exaggeration (which sometimes seems to be happening). Things are more complicated by the fact that *Gentlemen Prefer Blondes* is itself a comedy, itself mocking and exaggerating certain patriarchal gender roles. The situation is further confused by occasional play with the image in the video, destroying even the illusion of the stability of the stage/set space: at least once, a two-shot of Madonna II and one of the lovers is simply flipped over, in standard rock video style but in total violation of classical codes that seek to secure illusionism.

Since there is no diegetic audience, the spectator is now in direct rapport with Madonna's body, as she performs for the TV spectator. There is again no diegetic source of enunciation; the spectator either remains disoriented, or secures a position through the body of the historical star, Madonna, implied as "producing" the video or simply fixed on as a centering force. This is an issue to be taken up shortly.

Most of the camera work in the dance sequence involves sharp images and either long shots (the camera follows Madonna II's movements around the stage) or straight cuts; but towards the end of the dance rehearsal, the style changes to superimpositions and deliberately blurry shots, suggestive perhaps of a heightened eroticism. The camera allows Madonna II's head to be carried by the men underneath itself, so that only her arm remains in view; after some "dazed" shots, the camera pans left along the edge of the set to discover brown stairs with the D standing by them, gazing at the performance. But once again, the sequence was not set up, as it would have been in conventional Hollywood codes, as his structuring gaze; the gaze is only discovered *after* the fact, thus allowing enunciative confusion.

The same disorientation continues in a shot (perhaps a flash forward, although that term suggests the kind of narrative coherence that is precisely missing here) that follows after another dance sequence. Here the D is seen bringing simple daisies to a now smiling and receptive Madonna I, clothed in white (a play on Hollywood signifiers for innocence?), in her dressing room. We cut to the end of the stage performance (there are repeated blurry shots as before, again signifying, perhaps, sexual delirium), before a final cut to the space outside the studio, where the D is seen paying someone for the loan of a car. As Madonna I walks seductively out of the studio, the D ushers her into his car. The last shot is taken through the now rain-sodden glass (inexplicable diegetically) and shows their embrace.

This brief analysis of the main shots and use of diegetic spaces demonstrates the ways in which conventions of the classic Hollywood film, which paradoxically provided the inspiration for the video, are routinely violated. The purpose here was to show how even in a video that at first appears precisely to remain within those conventions – unlike many other videos whose extraordinary and avant-garde techniques are immediately obvious – regular narrative devices are not adhered to. But the video violates classic traditions even more with its sound—image relations.

This aspect of the video brings up the question of the rock video's uniqueness as an artistic form, namely as a form in which the sound of the song, and the "content" of its lyrics, is prior to the creation of images to accompany the music and the words. While there are

123

analogies to both the opera and to the Hollywood musical, neither form prepares for the rock video in which the song–image relationship is quite unique. The uniqueness has to do with a certain arbitrariness of the images used along with any particular song, with the lack of limitations spatially, with the frequently extremely rapid montage-style editing not found generally (if at all) in the Hollywood musical song/dance sequences, and finally with the precise relationship of sound – both musical and vocal – to image. This relationship involves (a) the links between musical rhythms and significations of instrumental sounds, and images provided for them; (b) links between the significations of the song's actual *words* and images conjured up to convey that "content"; (c) links between any one musical phrase and the accompanying words, and the relay of images as that phrase is being played and sung.

This is obviously a very complex topic – far beyond my scope here – but let me demonstrate some of the issues in relation to "Material Girl," where again things are far simpler than in many videos. We have seen that on the visual track there are two distinct but linked discourses, that involving the D's desire for Madonna I (his determined pursuit and eventual "winning" of her), and that of Madonna I's performance, where she plays Madonna II, the "material girl." These discourses are not hierarchically arranged as in the usual Hollywood film, but rather exist on a horizontal axis, neither subordinated to the other. In terms of screen time, however, the performance is given more time.

When we turn to the soundtrack, we find that, after the brief introductory scene in the screening room (a scene, by the way, often cut from the video), the soundtrack consists entirely of the lyrics for the song "Material Girl." This song deals with the girl who will only date boys who "give her proper credit," and for whom love is reduced to money. Thus, all the visuals pertaining to the D–Madonna I love story do not have any correlate on the soundtrack. We merely have two short verbal sequences (in the screening room and dressing room) to carry the entire other story: in other words, soundtrack and image track are not linked for that story. An obvious example of this discrepancy is the shot of Madonna I (arriving at the studio in the flashy car) rejecting her rich lover: Madonna lip-synches "That's right" from the "Material Girl" song – a phrase that refers

124

there to her only loving boys who give her money – in a situation where the opposite is happening: she *refuses* to love the man who is wealthy!

In other words, the entire video is subordinated to the words with their signifieds that refer in fact only to the stage performance. The common device in the Hollywood musical of having the dance inter-lude simply an episode in the main story seems here to be reversed: the performance is central while the love story is reduced to the status merely of a framing narrative. Significant here also is the disjunction between the two stories, the framing story being about a "nice" girl, and the performance being about the "bad" girl: but even these terms are blurred by the obvious seductiveness of the "nice" girl, particularly as she walks at the end toward the car in a very knowing manner.

We see thus that the usual hierarchical arrangement of discourses in the classical realist text is totally violated in "Material Girl." While Madonna I is certainly set up as object of the D's desire, in quite classical manner, the text refuses to let her be controlled by that desire. This is achieved by unbalancing the relations between framing story and performance story so that Madonna I is over-ridden by her stage figure, Madonna II, the brash, gutsy "material girl." The line between "fiction" and "reality" within the narrative is thus blurred: this has severe consequences just because the two women are polar opposites.

In *Gentlemen Prefer Blondes*, on the other hand, no such confu-sion or discrepancy exists. From the start, Monroe's single-minded aim is to catch a rich man, and she remains fixed on that throughout. The function of her performance of "Diamonds Are a Girl's Best Friend" is partly simply to express what has been obvious to the spec-tator, if not to Esmond, all along; but also to let Esmond get the idea, were he smart enough. Lorelei sings a song that expresses her philosophy of life, but we are clear about the lines between the stage-fiction and the context of its presentation, and Monroe as a character in the narrative. Part of the confusion in the Madonna video comes about precisely because the scene of the performance is not made very clear and because the lines between the different spaces of the text are blurred.

The situation in "Material Girl" is even more problematic because

125

of the way that Madonna, as historical star subject, breaks through her narrative positions via her strong personality, her love of performing for the camera, her inherent energy and vitality. Madonna searches for the camera's gaze and for the TV spectator's gaze that follows it because she relishes being desired. The "roles" melt away through her unique presence and the narrative incoherence discussed above seems resolved in our understanding that Madonna herself, as historical subject, is the really "material girl."

It is perhaps Madonna's success in articulating and parading the desire to be desired in an unabashed, aggressive, gutsy manner (as against the self-abnegating urge to lose oneself in the male that is evident in the classical Hollywood film) that attracts the hordes of 12-year-old fans who idolize her and crowd her concerts. The amazing "look alike" Madonna contests (viz. a recent Macy's campaign in New York) and the successful exploitation of the weird Madonna style of dress by clothing companies attests to this idolatry. It is significant that Madonna's early style is a far cry from the conventional "patriarchal feminine" of the women's magazines – it is a cross between a bordello queen and a bag lady: young teenagers may use her as a protest against their mothers and the normal feminine while still remaining very much within those modes (in the sense of spending a lot of money, time, and energy on their "look"; the "look" is still crucial to their identities, still designed to attract attention, even if provocatively).

In some sense, then, Madonna represents the postmodern feminist heroine in that she combines unabashed seductiveness with a gutsy kind of independence. She is neither particularly male nor female identified, and seems mainly to be out for herself. This postmodern feminism is part of a larger postmodernist phenomenon which her video also embodies in its blurring of hitherto sacrosanct boundaries and polarities of the various kinds discussed. The usual bipolar categories – male/female, high art/pop art, film/TV, fiction/reality, private/public, interior/ exterior, etc. – simply no longer apply to "Material Girl."

This analysis of "Material Girl" has shown the ambiguity of enunciative positions within the video that in turn is responsible for the ambiguous representation of the female image. The positioning of a video like "Material Girl," moreover, within the 24-hour flow on this commercial MTV channel, allows us to see that it is *this* sort of ambiguous image that appears frequently, as against any other possible female images, such as the ones mentioned earlier, which are only rarely cycled. That the video was directed by a woman, Mary Lambert, does not affect this argument. I would not collapse biological sexuality and ideological position. The post-feminist ambiguous images are clearly the ones sponsors consider "marketable", since they are not only most frequently cycled but also propagated in the ad texts that are interspersed among the video texts.

But let me, as I noted earlier, "stop the flow" and look briefly at other female representations with their different kinds of gaze and enunciative stances. It is significant that some of the female rock stars just preceding Madonna, such as Cyndi Lauper, Donna Summer, and Pat Benatar, came in on the coat-tails of the 1970s feminist movement. Interestingly enough, however, in the early 1980s they reflected different aspects of the "new" woman, Lauper often taking a woman-identified stance, Summer an explicitly "feminist" one, and Benatar embodying the "tough-woman" image.

In accord with a dominant strand of 1970s American feminism, all three stars attempted to "give woman the voice." The videos made from their lyrics fall broadly into the "socially conscious" category on my chart (see Table 3 on p. 55), and are most often made in a comparatively conventional narrative/realist style. The exception is Lauper's first video, "Girls Just Want to Have Fun," which comments playfully on young women's resistance to the confining traditional roles that their parents still demand, and employs all kinds of deconstructive technical devices in making its point. Part of the video's humor comes from the contrast between the extremely banal but tuneful pop music track and the imaginative visual devices.

This video embodies what was a common theme in the early 1980s, namely a strong anti-parental sentiment, often expressed in deliberate ridicule of adults. (Lauper's "Girls" in fact featured her own mother, filmed in Lauper's own home and evidently agreeing to be stereotyped.) Lauper's next, and highly successful, video, "Time After Time," belongs in the romantic category. It has a vague feminist angle in the heroine's decision to leave her boyfriend, evidently inspired by Marlene Dietrich's (first) refusal of her lover in *Morocco*. But more obviously feminist is the (in its time unusual)

127

representation of a close mother—daughter bonding. The video intermingles the heroine's love for the man with her love for her mother, suggesting a pre-Oedipal quality to the love affair. When her boyfriend rejects her, she conjures up an image of her mother comforting her, which in turn evokes memories of earlier closeness with her mother (we have a shot of the two hugging in the obviously working-class kitchen). Insisting on leaving her lover, despite his pleas, the heroine stops to hug her mother once more on her way to the station and the mournful parting.

The problem with this sort of representation of the mother is that while it is gratifying to see close mother—daughter bonding in a video (there are increasingly few videos that deal with parents at all, let alone in any positive manner), the mother is presented in realist codes that cannot conceal her powerlessness. She comes across as an oppressed figure, pathetic, weak even. Peripheral to the narrative as usual, she cannot help her daughter, merely commiserating rather than taking control or bringing about change. (Paradoxically, some of the videos in the romantic category by male stars, such as Paul Young's "Every Time You Go Away," may open up new space precisely through avoiding any literal representation of the mother. Addressed as an absent figure, the mother-surrogate's gaze is nevertheless inscribed in such videos in a way that makes itself more powerfully experienced than in literal images.)

Similar problems beset the more explicitly feminist video by Donna Summer, "She Works Hard for the Money," shown in 1983. This hard-hitting video makes explicit its political message about woman's oppression. It focuses on a working-class woman's double jeopardy as single working parent, oppressed both within the home and in the job. The video's textual strategies are largely realist, except that the story is narrated rather untraditionally by Summer herself, in the position of "host," conducting the viewer through the heroine's daily life. Summer "shows" us how she has to work two jobs, do all the housework, and put up in addition with two quarrelsome, ungrateful kids. The images reveal the heroine in one appalling situation after another, there being no respite, while "Summer" as it were provides a didactic "reading" of the images as exemplifying woman's lot. The only mitigating aspects to the misery are our host's personal solidarity with the heroine (but since she is out-

Pat Benatar, "Love is a Battlefield"

Led by the heroine, the women in the bordello march out onto the street protesting their treatment. The "tough-woman" image is combined unselfconsciously with pleasurable aspects of the patriarchal feminine.

side the diegesis she cannot help her!), and the final scene in which all kinds of women, from different professions, gather together on the street to dance. It is a nice but utopian moment, resolving in a fantasized solidarity what in fact requires concrete *social* change.

Pat Benatar's far more successful and frequently cycled "Love is a Battlefield" embodies Benatar's tough-woman stance. (Benatar in an interview criticized most female stars for their self-denigrating romantic preoccupations, the "If you leave me, I'll die" syndrome; she herself prefers the "If you leave me, I'll kick your ass" stance. This explains, she noted, her finding male stars far more interesting than female ones!) Benatar's early video exposes the limitations of the nuclear family – the heroine is thrown out of her home at the start – and reveals woman's vulnerabilities in the big city. Ending up as a prostitute, the heroine nevertheless takes action against the male oppressing her friend; once again, the women side with one another, marching bravely out of the brothel to engage in a war-like, threatening dance on the street outside before going their separate ways.

The difference between these two "feminist" videos explains the relative success of the latter, as against the short cycling of the first. For the female representations in Benatar's video almost belie the strong woman-identified theme in their reliance on the standard "look" of the patriarchal feminine: the heroine, played by Benatar herself, is particularly glamorous, and the prostitutes' clothes, while somewhat unconventional, are colorful and fetching.

These videos are all important in offering alternate female narrative/thematic positions, if not alternate images. This distinction is important, since it reveals the limitation of a traditional liberal-humanist feminist politics expressed through fairly conventional filmic codes. Madonna's most recent video (August 1986), "Papa Don't Preach," is interesting in this connection, since it shows Madonna evolving a kind of postmodern feminist image that builds on, or combines, elements of the "new" woman that we traced in Summer, Lauper, and Benatar. This image, unlike her previous ones (of which "Material Girl" gives a glimpse), smacks not so much of post-modernism (although categories are still blurred in some ways) as of a combination of pre-feminist modes with ones we might call "feminist." In "Papa Don't Preach" (top of the countdown in America for a second week in August 1986, after having already

Madonna, "Papa Don't Preach"

Madonna keeps the virgin/whore dichotomy intact but reworks it in the
body of a single protagonist.

Madonna's new *gamin* image

131

made the top in most European nations), the heroine is a determined, self-asserting teenager who, having fallen in love and become pregnant, insists on keeping her baby. Madonna's image is far removed from the bordello Queen/bag lady mix of her recent period; now svelt, almost gamin-like in her short hair cut, she struts confidently along in jeans and striped top as the video opens. These images of the home girl, *Daddy*'s girl indeed, it turns out, (the heroine seems to have been brought up by her father, there being no mother-image in the video), are intercut with images of the "bad" girl – although she is not really labelled as such – dressed in skin-tight black pants and 1950s-style black corset top, which sets off her blonde hair, white face, and bright red lips. She dances erotically in these scenes, and her words suggest the "bad" girl: "Papa don't preach," she begins, addressing her father, "I'm in trouble deep/I've been losing sleep/But I made up my mind/I'm keeping my baby." But it is precisely the blurring of the lines between the "virgin" and "whore" images that suggest a post-feminist stance; the heroine is *neither*, but rather a sexy young teenager, in love and pregnant, and refusing to conform to social codes and give up her baby (as her friends, she says, tell her to do).

But this postmodern feminist heroine still wants to be Daddy's girl: "Papa, don't stop loving me" she says. The last scene of the video involves the gradual reconciliation of father and daughter, the final shot being their embrace. It is important, however, that the reconciliation only happens because the *father* decides to relent, the heroine simply refusing to be what he demands; she insists on being herself.

As the video's rapid and broad success suggests, Madonna has here touched on issues confronting many teenagers today, particularly those in the lower classes, which her video (set as it is in a section of New Jersey facing New York City's skyline) obviously addresses. It shows a star evolving, perhaps maturing as a result of her own much-publicized recent marriage. Madonna is here far less seductive toward her audience, much more direct and forceful. She is at once strong and feminine, sexy and "innocent," offering an image that perhaps makes sense to young women growing up after the recent feminist movement.

Nevertheless, the video has some of the same problems as those by Summer, Lauper, and Benatar already discussed in that its (broadly)

132

realist strategies prevent any foregrounding of problems of female representation. Madonna pastes the traditional virgin onto the traditional whore, hoping to get rid of a polarity that no longer makes sense. But in not questioning the polarity's very terms, she runs the risk of keeping it intact. Perhaps because of their (essentially) liberal-humanist politics, these female stars have been less ready to experiment with aesthetic forms than have male stars. (It is significant that most of the prize-winning experimental videos have been produced by male video directors for male stars or groups such as The Cars, Dire Straits, Simple Minds, Phil Collins, David Bowie, Mick Jagger, Michael Jackson, Rush, The Power Station, A-Ha. This is not to deny the artistically innovative work of a Laurie Anderson or a Mary Lambert (or directors like Annabel Jankel or Tony Basil). It is a matter of what is given institutional acclaim. The list reflects the dominance of white male figures in the rock video phenomenon.

It is precisely women's position in the male order that is addressed in Tina Turner's effective "Private Dancer." This video, instead of presenting an explicit feminist message in the manner of Benatar's and Summer's videos, rather attempts to expose woman's position in the dominant male imaginary. It analyzes the structure of a male unconscious that reduces women to mere cyphers, signs in a male discourse, or instruments of pleasure shaped to satisfy male fantasies.

The video's enunciative strategies work to deconstruct the male imaginary: the heroine, played by Turner herself, is first seen in a realist image entering the high class bordello where she tells us, through the song lyrics, that she works as a "private dancer." Turner continues to speak this video as she moves from being a realistic character to a kind of female "metteur en scène," or a magician, conjuring up different aspects of the male erotic unconscious. Dressed now in elegant evening gown, Turner addresses the camera directly, in close-up or medium-shot, but the angles diminish fetishization of her form. She speaks here of the performer's own life and hopes – the need for money that brings her here, the wish for a family, home, and fun – the video aiming to construct a disjunction between "woman" and "male fantasy."

From this position, the heroine creates for the TV viewer the dream world of her clients, but in such a way as to highlight the

133

oppressiveness of the fantasies imposed on the women in the bordello. The actresses and dancers participating in the fantasies are made to perform like robots or mannequins, reduced to mere mechanical embodiments of what men desire. Sometimes, the figures are seen to be operated like puppets, by ribbons tied to their limbs. They are seen to be at the command of the male customer, to produce the required image as would a machine.

The video's visual techniques produce the effect of a dream-space: one male fantasy, performed by the robot-like, mechanical figures, is made to merge into the next, the camera often floating in on a scene, watching it for a while until the image dissolves into another, when the camera will float out again. The effect is that of swooning, or of a dream-world in which anything can happen and in which one is not in control. The mise-en-scène adds further to the dream-like quality through the veils and netting that are draped across the image and through the claustrophobic sense of being in an enclosed, artificial space.

Tina Turner, "Private Dancer"

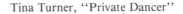

Turner uses her body to construct a meta-language for us to see *how* women are mere passive objects of male desire.

134

Some of the fantasies conjured up involve the heroine herself, so that we get the double articulation of her narration outside of the male fantasies she conducts us through, and her positioning within those fantasies. The result is our understanding her physical/bodily ensnarement within the male imaginary, but experiencing her psychic detachment from it.

It is this representation of a psychic detachment that permits the exposing of the male erotic unconscious. The video constructs a kind of meta-language within which to let us see *how* the heroine's body is (ab)used, *how* women are mere passive objects of male desire, entrapped within a male fantasy world from which there is no escape. The blocking of woman's subjectivity and of her own desires is graphically depicted.

The video ends as it began with the realist image of the dance hall where clients and customers first meet. We have seen that this is a space controlled by the ever-watching Madame, making sure that her "dancers" are doing their job of pleasing the clients. The heroine is shot in close-up with her client and then, suddenly, seen to push him away and walk off the floor as the video ends.

This moment of negation of her role exposes the pathetic degree of resistance available to the woman. She cannot *change* anything, or free herself of the male constructions; she can only walk away from the scene, temporarily take herself out of the role.

While race is absent as any overt part of the narrative in "Private Dancer," it perhaps accounts for the video's uncanny ability to present what is a predominantly white male imaginary. The only overt reference to race is perhaps the brief scene where a young beautifully dressed black boy and girl are seen dancing together; the little boy suddenly gets bored and walks away from the now-forlorn little girl. Perhaps the scene indicates the enmeshment of young black children in white codes; or the early vulnerability of the girl to seduction and betrayal? It is unclear.

This video is quite different from others produced for Turner, and its Turner-image is unusual. A number of videos were made from her very successful and remarkably staged London performance, where she unabashedly promoted her body as a sexual commodity. On the other hand, one can argue that in a video like "What's Love Got To Do With It" Turner attempts to gain control over her own

Tina Turner, "What's Love Got To Do With It?"

Turner and other black stars like Aretha Franklin initiated the "tough woman" stance being modified by new black singers. Here Turner comes between the heterosexual couple, "rescuing" the woman being seduced.

Turner appropriates the patriarchal feminine for herself as a strategy for retaining control over her desirability and keeping her independence.

136

sexuality through deliberately enticing male desire. Her short tight leather skirt with the slit up the side, her bestockinged legs and high-heeled shoes are in this case arguably used simply to assert control over the males by refusing them what her dress seems to offer. Turner here comes close to Benatar's "tough-woman" image, seeming to ask women to band together rather than giving in to male desire. But this is again merely a position taken up in the one lyric from which this video was made.

Turner's most recent video, "Typical Male," (August 1986) still assumes a "tough woman" image, but now Turner is poking fun at the intellectual male to whom she's attracted but from whom she cannot get "a reaction." She positions herself as trying to entice the male, with little success. The video plays off of the idea of Turner's enormous sexual desirability, rendering ridiculous the male who doesn't seem to notice it. Dressed in a strapless red dress and high heels, she parades about the set full of giant-size symbols of intellectuality (crossword puzzles, paper, pencils, chessboard, etc.) Her pleading position ("All I want is a little reaction/Just enough to tip the scale"; and "So put up your books . . . /Open up your heart and let me in") at once belittles her (she is literally pint-sized amongst the huge symbols of male intellect), and paradoxically emasculates and ridicules the reluctant (weak) male. The result is a strange mixture of the different kinds of address in the earlier videos discussed above.

Julie Brown's "The Homecoming Queen's Got a Gun," only shown a few times, deconstructs a staple of American mythology. This Homecoming Queen revolts against all that is expected of her, in the mode of a kind of black comedy. Bodies litter the house where she starts shooting, and of course, she is in turn shot by the police. The video's iconoclasm is powerful and disturbing, but the extreme rebellion against an oppressive female role perhaps prevented the video from being shown more often.

The last variation from the prevalent "post-feminist" female representation that I will deal with in my stopping of the 24-hour MTV flow is that evident in the recent Aretha Franklin/Annie Lennox "Sisters Are Doin' It For Themselves" video. The female images here are arguably different from those in either the feminist-message video or the deconstructive Turner video. At first glance, the Franklin/Lennox video looks like the feminist-message type, but on a closer

137

examination the video attempts to move beyond the mere often romantic celebration of women's achievements that it does include.

There is first the amazing contrast between the images of the two star subjects themselves, who perform on a huge outdoor stage before crowds of ethnically mixed female fans. Franklin's image is embedded in discourses of the historically "strong" black female blues singer, as well as those of the black, no-nonsense matriarch. Her image is now frequent on MTV — as she appears in her own successful videos, as a co-star in this "Sisters" video; or as a homage-image in Whitney Houston's 'How Will I Know." Lennox, meanwhile, typifies the new androgynous rock-video discourse which is largely, however, a male phenomenon. Here she is resplendent in white male-style jacket, black leather pants, heavy boots, and short cropped blonde hair. Franklin, meanwhile, performs in a simple red gown. There is thus a bringing together of powerful, current, alternative female images and the past strength of black female discourses.

These different images of the female are also developed in the cut-aways from the two women performing and the montage sequences of shots of women spliced together. These intercut shots are of three main kinds: those showing women in non-traditional jobs, from presidents to construction workers; those showing women in the old patriarchal "feminine" rituals such as the traditional Indian marriage or the cheer-leader; and, finally, clips from silent films and those like Schlesinger's *A Kind of Loving* or Vidor's *Our Daily Bread* which show women as classic sex objects or idealized mother figures.

This montage sequence reminds the female viewer of where women have been and of where they have gotten to, but the inter-mixing of the various sets of images suggests the continuity of the old positions along with the new. There is thus an attempt to avoid the utopian element of the feminist message video by showing the series on a continuum rather than in a clear past versus present hier-archical ordering.

Most interesting perhaps is what the video does with the image of Dave Stewart played upon a huge screen that appears between the images of Lennox and Franklin on stage towards the end of the video. At first, one is perturbed at his presence at all in such a celebration of women's achievements; but it soon becomes clear that the video is using his image to say something about the processes of image-making already raised in the montage clips from male films. Here it appears that instead of the usual control of the female image by the male gaze, Stewart's image is being controlled by Lennox and Franklin as they stand on either side of the screen depicting his image. It is almost as if they are pulling some strings to make the image move in certain ways, much as the women in Turner's video were "operated" by the male unconscious. Stewart's figure is very much positioned as the object of the women's gazes, and further is reduced to a kind of mechanical object as it bounces about apparently uncontrollably within the screen.

Finally, there is an interesting attempt in the video to avoid making Franklin and Lennox direct objects of the camera's gaze. While there are inevitably some close-ups of their faces, for much of the time the camera catches them at oblique angles, so that their gazes do not directly meet the camera's. At times, this creates an unfortunate sense of their not-relating to each other, but this is in the service of avoiding an objectifying gaze as much as possible.

This video then appears to comment upon the problems of image-making and to foreground the notion that images are constructed rather than "natural." It processes old and new female constructions as if to warn us both of too readily assuming that old images have been abandoned and of the fact that women have currently been newly constructed as "liberated" or whatever. The present of the video, i.e. that of the concert where Franklin and Lennox are apparently performing, does convey a sense of female solidarity and celebration in the old utopian mode. However, there is a certain self-consciousness about this mode, as is evident in its presentation as yet one more "image." This is conveyed through the device of projecting, on a huge screen within the frame, images of Franklin and Lennox and the concert we are watching, intercut with images from the montage sequence of women shown earlier on in the video.

"Sisters" only got very short play on MTV, seemingly having made it that far merely because it was top of the British charts. As we resume the 24-hour flow, so such alternate female images once again recede into the background and the post-feminist image reappears.

As I noted earlier, the postmodern as an "ideology" has recently

139

begun to shift all the hitherto quite distinct types in the same direction. So the fact that the post-feminist video is the dominant one in the flow is only to be expected. Nevertheless, there are videos that may be said to belong in a separate category, that may still be distinguished from the others as embodying in extreme form what they now merely show by an *inflection* into their hitherto specific type. Let me conclude this chapter by a brief look at some postmodernist videos which, unlike the majority of other types, seem to reflect Baudrillard's notion that, while the psychological is marked, "it seems to be played out somewhere else."

As we have seen, there are two main types of gaze – pre-Oedipal and phallic – in the other types of video. While the way these gazes function in at least two of the types differs markedly from the gaze in the classical narrative film, it nevertheless can still be usefully discussed within the psychoanalytic paradigm. This is not the case in the postmodernist video because of the refusal of the text to speak from any definite position. A video like Devo's "Whip It," for example, not only blurs distinctions between genres but refuses to reveal that it is speaking from a clear position. The issue of the gaze thus becomes confused: we have a sense of the text playing with Oedipal positionings but not really adopting any of them. The predominance of the pastiche mode makes it difficult to say that the video is taking the usual phallic pleasure in violence to women, although the surface imagery would suggest such pleasure.

The video sets itself back in the "mythic" West, toward which it takes a stand somewhere between pastiche and parody. There is intercutting between the band, dressed in extraordinary clothes that are a mix between children's television "Pot Men" and *Star-Trek* and standing in some obviously artificial TV garden plot, and a group of cowboys and cowgals, joking at the side of an open space. On this space stands what looks at first like a wax figure of a woman, dressed in old-fashioned middle-class women's clothes. As the band play and sing, the star whips the clothes off the woman, piece by piece. We see her body gradually becoming naked, the clothes flying off her as she is whipped; meanwhile, the cowboy group laugh at the display, and we cut to a fat/ugly Mom figure in a nearby house window, stirring her mixture and taking pleasure in her son's temerity. A comic-bubble out of her mouth has in it the words "Oh that Alan!"

140

GENDER ADDRESS AND THE GAZE

This video perplexes because the spectator is not provided with any clear place from which to identify. The pastiche element confuses: we want to believe that this is parody, but that is never made clear; if it is not parody, what is meant? Does the video want to have its cake and eat it too – that is, at once mock violence toward women while clearly itself quite enjoying what it shows? The female spectator has absolutely no position to occupy, torn as she is between disbelief and an unavoidable pity for the figure of the woman in the center. The representation of the fat/ugly complicit Mom further angers the female spectator, while at the same time she fears that she is being trapped by "taking it seriously," when the video might be a comment on the macho nature of the West!

Tom Petty and the Heartbreakers, "Don't Come Around Here No More"

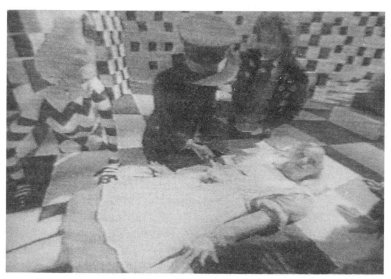

Like other postmodernist videos, this one refuses to speak from a clear position. Is the eating of Alice's body sadistic or a play with sadistic wishes?

Another video, with a similarly ambiguous pastiche mode, is Tom Petty and the Heartbreakers' "Don't Come Around Here No More," which is based on the Alice story. A very imaginatively filmed tape, with fantastic set, creative camera use, costumes, and special effects (particularly the sudden size transformations of Alice and the Mad Hatter, and of objects like her tea cup), it is nevertheless chilling in its treatment of Alice and her body. The Mad Hatter has apparently turned into a sadist, with not a grain of humor; he is cruelly rejecting of Alice, briefly playing with her (making himself suddenly tiny, spouting mirrors like ears in which she sees her own image), and then sadistically taunting her. He has food brought to her, but then his servants steal it; he seats her at the table, but then rushes toward her and knocks her down; he sends a pram her way, only for her to discover an ugly piglet under the baby bonnet, and finally all but drowns her in his now huge tea cup, scaring her with the ringed faces of his servants peering down at her; the Hatter chases her around and finally he ends by cutting up her body, now mysteriously transformed into birthday cake, and eating it.

As with "Whip It," this video simply refuses to speak from any clear position. How are we to view the eating of Alice's body? It may seem "sadistic," but the rest of the filmic world does not really support such a reading. The events do not have the overall investment in a certain kind of desire that the sadistic narrative usually has. The narrative rather plays with sadistic wishes without really declaring them, leaving the viewer perplexed as to how to read the images.

Let me now discuss the similar kind of perplexity that an attempt to evaluate the channel as a whole produces and that seems particularly to indicate postmodernism.

6

Conclusion: MTV, postmodernism, and the televisual apparatus

In this book, I have tried to argue that MTV, as a 24-hour continuous channel, carries to an extreme, and thus lays bare for our contemplation, aspects inherent in the televisual apparatus. To summarize the main points in that argument briefly: first, the main force of MTV as a cable channel is consumption on a whole variety of levels, ranging from the literal (i.e. selling the sponsors' goods, the rock stars' records, and MTV itself) to the psychological (i.e. selling the image, the "look," the style). MTV is more obviously than other programs one nearly continuous advertisement, the flow being merely broken down into different *kinds* of ads. More than other programs, then, MTV positions the spectator in the mode of constantly hoping that the next ad-segment (of whatever kind) will satisfy the desire for plenitude: the channel keeps the spectator in the consuming mode more intensely because its items are all so short.

Since the mode of address throughout is that of the ad, then like the ad the channel relies on engaging the spectator on the level of unsatisfied desire. This remains in the psyche from the moment of entry into the Lacanian symbolic, and is available for channeling in various directions. Given the organization of the Lacanian symbolic around the phallus as signifier, it is not surprising that MTV basically addresses the desire for the phallus remaining in the psyche of both genders. This partly accounts for the dominance on the channel of videos featuring white male stars.

143

Second, we have seen how the fact that MTV calls into question hitherto sacrosanct aesthetic and critical polarities marks MTV as a postmodernist form. Its very status as a commercial form using avant-garde techniques has required a re-examination of previous critical categories.

Third, we have seen how the position that MTV takes toward history again marks its discourse as postmodernist. In a postmodernist fashion, MTV blurs previous distinctions between past, present, and future, along with its blurring of separations such as those between popular and avant-garde art, between different aesthetic genres and artistic modes. MTV, as a text, arguably makes a postmodernist use of historical discourses about rock and roll as constructed by rock critics.[1] We saw how there are four main phases of rock and roll – the beginnings in the 1950s with Bill Haley, Elvis Presley, and numerous other groups like Chuck Berry, the Platters, etc.; the 1960s "soft rock," often influenced by black "soul" music and jazz; the late 1960s so-called "acid rock," which for many represents the height of genuine rock and roll, with its inventive sounds and protest content; the 1970s search for new sounds in the wake of the collapse of youth and protest movements, leading in the 1980s to punk, heavy metal, and new wave rock and roll, with their loud, unmelodious sounds, their cynicism, their negative violence.

Each phase has been seen as addressing distinct historical teenage communities, distinguished by dress and by stance toward the establishment. MTV, however, simply sweeps up these discourses and distinctions into itself, calling upon all the separate traditions, re-shaping and re-using them for its own ends, flattening them out into one continuous present of the 24-hour video flow. MTV also effaces the boundary between past and present in drawing indiscriminately on film genres and art movements from different historical periods; and also in the often arbitrary use of settings and clothes from the Roman, medieval and other past eras. The stance of the texts is that there is one time continuum in which all exists: past, present, and future do not indicate major time barriers, but rather a time band upon which one can call at will.

Now what is interesting here is the way in which this timeless present often has a futurist, post-holocaust look, even when a video is not explicitly drawing upon science fiction, or using footage from

144

CONCLUSION

futurist films like Lang's *Metropolis, Star-Trek* or the more recent
Blade Runner. We already saw this in some of the nihilist videos
analyzed in detail (particularly "Rebel Yell" and "Rock You Like a
Hurricane"), but the phenomenon is common across the types. Most
often the rock video world looks like noplace, or like a post-nuclear
holocaust place – without boundaries, definition or recognizable
location. Figures are often placed in a smoky, hazy environment
and, as already noted, the sudden, unexplained explosion is a common feature.

Marxist critics like Fredric Jameson and Lawrence Grossberg
object to the fact – evidenced by this stance toward history – that
postmodernist texts like MTV refuse to take up a secure critical position from which to speak. As critics who themselves retain a notion
of history as manifesting a position of "truth" about the world,
rather than yet one more discourse, they view contemporary youth
culture as in danger because it does not take an explicitly critical
stance toward on-going events.

Rock and roll is vulnerable to this objection because of some of
the subversive roots (first from slave songs, then jazz, and finally
1960s protest rock) that form the basic traditions for all rock music.
But elements of rock have long "sold out" to commercial entrepre-
neurs; the line between rock and pop has always been tentative,
"pop" always attempting to bring the more rebellious "rock" into
the mainstream.

But Jameson and Grossberg are correct in pointing out that a
more fundamental change is taking place than the *mere* commercialization that MTV signifies. The stance toward history represents a
new era, emblematic of the Baudrillardean "Universe of Communication"; for it is the televisual apparatus that is partly responsible
for the kind of consciousness that no longer thinks in terms of an
historical frame. That sort of "frame" involves precisely the kinds
of boundaries and limited texts that television obliterates in its
never-ending series.

In eliding history as a position from which to speak, rock videos
fall into pastiche rather than parody, as we've seen, signifying a new
lack of orienting boundaries, a tendency to incorporate rather than
to "quote" texts. Without drawing the negative judgments about
postmodernism that Jameson does, we can see that MTV is part of a

contemporary discourse that has written out history as a possible discourse. What are the implications of this? To what degree is the cultural situation, as evident in MTV, progressive or dangerous, transgressive or regressive?

Marxist critics tend to draw negative conclusions: Jameson, for instance, is concerned about what he calls a new schizophrenic mode of relating to the world. Building on work by Lacan and Baudrillard, Jameson sees this as an inevitable product of the stance toward history. "The originality of Lacan's thought in this area," Jameson notes, "is to have considered schizophrenia essentially as a language disorder. . . . What we need to retain from this is the idea that psychosis, and more particularly schizophrenia, emerges from the failure of the infant to accede fully into the realm of speech and language."[2] This enables us to see schizophrenia as "the breakdown of the relationship between signifiers." Jameson notes that for Lacan, the experience of temporality – of past, present, and future – and of an identity that persists over time is an effect of language, produced through the fact that the sentence moves through time, linearly.[3] But since the schizophrenic does not recognize the time element in langauge, he/she does not have a sense of time as continuous. She/he, says Jameson:

> is condemned to live in a perpetual present with which the various moments of his or her past have little connection and for which there is no conceivable future on the horizon. . . . The schizophrenic experience is an experience of isolated, disconnected, discontinuous material signifiers which fail to link up into a coherent sequence.[4]

Jameson goes on to note that "as temporal continuities break down, the experience of the present becomes powerfully, overwhelmingly vivid and 'material.'" What he means here is that because the schizophrenic cannot experience in words their larger contextual and temporal meanings, so she/he focuses in on their literality, their presentness, their sensory elements, not seeking to look beyond to broader signification.[5]

What is disturbing to Jameson about this is that the previous modernist movement at least retained a critical position vis-à-vis dominant culture, whereas society now takes into itself whatever

146

is produced from a counter-culture, such as punk rock and sexually explicit material. Far from this material being condemned by the establishment, it is rather made into a successful commercial commodity. Fashion, styling, advertising, etc., are all fed by postmodernism in an unprecedented manner. The problem with this, for Jameson, is the "disappearance of a sense of history" and the living "in a perpetual present and in a perpetual change that obliterates traditions of the kind which all earlier social formations have had in some way or another to preserve."[6]

While Jameson is concerned about the loss of any critical position from which to evaluate contemporary developments, Grossberg is obsessed with the negativity of recent punk rock music. He sees the despair and nihilism that stalks the music as representing the impossibility of youth to challenge, or hope to change, existing social formations from which they are, however, alienated. Rock and roll in the 1980s, Grossberg notes, "is no longer able to constitute itself a powerful affective boundary between its fans and those who remain outside of its culture. . . . Survival for this new youth seems to demand adaptation to and escape from, the hegemony rather than a response to the historical context in which they find themselves."[7] The moment leans dangerously deathward for Grossberg.

A more positive reading of MTV would involve linking it to a radical kind of postmodernism such as has emerged recently from theoretical developments in France. In its radical, Derridean form, postmodernism embodies an attack on bourgeois signifying practices. As a critical theory, postmodernism exposes how these practices, posing as speaking what is "natural" and "true," in fact set up a transcendental self as a point outside of articulation. But the practices conceal this point of enunciation, which is that of bourgeois hegemony, so that the spectator is unaware of being addressed from a particular position. The postmodernist critic and artist use radically transgressive forms in an effort to avoid the false illusionist position of a speaker outside of articulation. The "freeing" of the signifiers is in this case a kind of strategy – a way of preventing their usual linkage to mythic signifieds. The decentering of the spectator/reader then has a radical effect in releasing him/her from predictable, confining signifieds.

From this perspective, one could see the effacing in MTV of old boundaries between low and high culture, between past, present, and future, and between previously distinct art forms and genres as an exhilarating move toward a heteroglossia that calls into question moribund pieties of a now archaic humanism. The refusal of classical continuity editing, of the normal cause—effect narrative progression, of shot/counter-shot, of time—place unities makes new demands on the spectator, requiring a more active involvement; videos provide a whole variety of filmic worlds, as against the monolithic world of the classical realist Hollywood film. The creativity and energy of rock videos could represent a refusal to be co-opted into the liberalism that has brought America to its present crisis.

Far from the incoherent flow of images signaling a schizophrenic failure of language, the young adult's refusal to enter the realm of the symbolic could represent a healthy breaking of confining boundaries and dichotomies that were constructed originally to serve certain bourgeois ends at a particular historical moment. In this view, then, the vitality of rock videos shows the refusal of youth to be silenced or channeled in the old directions.

The very possibility of such contradictory readings of MTV is, again, part of what marks it as postmodernist. The institution is itself embedded in contradictions that are an inevitable part of its cultural context. There is some truth to the reading of MTV as a merely co-opted kind of postmodernism that utilizes adolescent desire for its own, commercial ends. The adoption of adolescent styles, imagery, and iconography by the adult fashion and advertising worlds, by TV shows like *Miami Vice* and by Hollywood films, does not necessarily signal a healthy acceptance of youth's subversive stances; it rather suggests the cynicism by which profit has become the *only* value – a cynicism represented by spies like Michael Walker trading secrets not for *ideological* but merely for monetary reasons.

We need to distinguish this co-opted postmodernism, which seeks to contain its possibly progressive decentering effects, from the radical Derridean kind. The Derridean decentering is ultimately unpleasurable because it refuses the plenitude and unity we all desire, and that makes us vulnerable to dominant commercial forms that tap into this need with their complicit ideologies. MTV at once addresses the American adolescent's consciousness of a decentered world,

148

while also providing a longed-for centeredness in the faces and bodies of the rock stars.

Contradictions abound in the representation of sexuality on MTV, as we've seen. As I have shown, the male gaze is not monolithic on the channel: here again, the televisual apparatus enables the production of a variety of different gazes due to the arrangement of a series of short, constantly changing segments in place of the two-hour continuous film narrative, or the usually single book-length or theatrical narratives. There is no possibility within the four-minute segment (others are shorter) for regression to the Freudian Oedipal conflicts in the manner of the classical narrative. What we rather have is a semi-comical play with Oedipal positions, as in the postmodern video, or a focus on one particular mode in the Oedipal complex in some of the other video-types outlined in Chapter 5.

The implications of all this for a feminist perspective need close analysis. Feminism has traditionally relied on a liberal or left humanist position, as was clear in my earlier discussion of major types of videos featuring female stars. If the televisual apparatus manifests a new stage of consciousness in which that liberal/left humanism no longer has a place, this implicates a majority of feminist positions. If Baudrillard is correct in seeing the TV screen as symbolizing a new era in which "The Faustian, Promethean (perhaps Oedipal) period of production and consumption" has given way to "the narcissistic and protean era of connections, contact, contiguity, feedback, and generalized interface that goes with the universe of communication," then feminism needs to address the changed situation. Gender has been one of the central organizing categories of what Baudrillard has called the old "hot" (as against the new "cold") universe, but this may be lost in the new era. Let me explore briefly what the impact of this might be for women and feminism.

Women's patriarchal functions have been constructed historically through the patriarchal institutions and social codes that Marx and Freud found in operation and around which they each, in different ways, constructed authoritative discourses in the late nineteenth and early twentieth centuries. One might think that the demise of the institutions that gave rise to these discourses would automatically benefit women. But this is not necessarily the case.

For, while the postmodernism that is partly produced by the

149

collapse of the old structures has some progressive aspects, it is a contradictory phenomenon for women. Contemporary feminism, as a political discourse, has developed a position from which to speak by attacking the old patriarchal theorists; feminists have both made use of and critiqued the powerful, often subversive, discourses of both Marx and Freud in their stance against dominant gender constructs. In other words, these discourses have provided the shaping framework for our work. If they are no longer relevant, on what ground does the feminist critique stand?

Second, as an aesthetic, postmodernism constructs a decentered, fragmented text; the breaking up of traditional, realist forms sometimes entails a deconstruction of conventional sex-role representations that opens up new possibilities for female imaging. Further, the fragmentation of the viewing subject perhaps deconstructs woman's conventional other-centered reception functions – women positioned as nurturer, care-giver – releasing new ways of relating to texts. Postmodernism offers the female spectator pleasure in sensations – color, sound, visual patterns – and in energy, body movement; it also opens up possibilities for expression of female desire.

On the other hand, one could argue that postmodernist culture primarily builds on and satisfies already dominant masculine qualities, such as violence, destruction, consumption, phallic sexuality, appropriation of the feminine in the non-male image. In postmodernism, as I've tried to show, often the domestic and the familial, especially the figure of the mother, are repressed; and these are modes that in the past offered some satisfactions to women. It is possible that the new "universe of communication" is precisely pleasing to males seeking relief from the old "Faustian, Promethean (perhaps Oedipal) period of production and consumption," just because women have begun, through their feminist discourse, to make and win demands within that system, thereby challenging male dominance there.

Is it possible that the postmodernist discourse has been constructed by male theorists partly to mitigate the increasing dominance of feminist theory in intellectual discourse? Could the discourse also partly remedy the gap in male theory resulting from the end of an era in French intellectual life, marked by the literal deaths of several of the great 1960s theorists — Jacques Lacan, Roland Barthes, Michel

CONCLUSION

Foucault and the withdrawal from the scene of Louis Althusser? I am not suggesting that the discourse does not accurately describe a new set of subject constructions produced by (and themselves producing, circularly) new technologies; indeed, my book has tried to show the links between one such new technology (i.e. television) and new subject constructions in rock videos. What I am suggesting is that certain theorists are drawn to postmodernism (rather than struggling against it) precisely because it seems to render feminism obsolete — because it offers a relief from the recent concentration on feminist discourse.

However this may be, it is important for feminists to confront the postmodernist challenge. Given television's role in the changed and still changing relationship of subject to image, feminists must analyze the implications of this postmodernist apparatus. The change involved began at the turn of the century with the development of advertising and of the department-store window; it was then further affected by the invention of the cinematic apparatus, and television has, we've seen, produced more changes. The television screen now replaces the cinema screen as the central controlling cultural mode, setting up a new spectator—screen relationship which I have begun to analyze in this book on MTV. For MTV constantly comments upon the self in relation to image (especially the TV image), to the extent that that may be seen as its main "content." The blurring of distinctions between a "subject" and an "image" – or the reduction of the old notion of "self" to "image" – is something for feminists to explore, even as we fear the coming of Baudrillard's universe of "simulacra."

The reduction of the female body to merely an "image" is something that women have lived with for a long time, and the phenomenon has been extensively studied by feminist film critics. But this study always somehow assumed an entity possible of being constructed differently. The new postmodern universe, with its celebration of the look, the surfaces, textures, the self-as-commodity, threatens to reduce everything to the image/representation/simulacrum.

Research is also needed on the impact of the televisual apparatus on other potentially oppositional discourses, such as those (like USA Africa, Live Aid, Farm Aid and, as of writing, Amnesty International) mentioned in Chapter 4. As one of America's powerful commercial apparatuses, television seems able to integrate and use any kind of potentially subversive counter-culture before it has even had time to identify itself as such. While this capacity of television (and, indeed, of American culture generally) may result in a certain humanizing of the dominant discourse – all to the good – it means that oppositional discourses are never given an opportunity to structure a community; once it existed, such a discourse shared by numbers of people might gain sufficient power to produce real changes in dominant discourses. (A good recent example is the "integration" of what had begun as an oppositional discourse about poverty in America, in the recent "Hands Across America" event, when Ronald Reagan finally agreed to let the line go through the White House and to stand in it himself.)

The loss of any position from which to speak – of mechanisms for critical evaluation of social structures and ideologies – that characterizes postmodernism is something to worry about even as we see the value of a radical postmodernism that moves beyond archaic humanism. While there may be a genuinely oppositional youth culture in some European nations, this is no longer true of America. What we have predominantly is a uni-dimensional, commercialized and massified youth culture, not really organized by youth itself but by commercial agents, that has absorbed into itself, and trivialized, all the potentially subversive positions of earlier rock movements. There are of course small sub-groups that are important but, just because marginalized and lacking access to the media, they are powerless. Any attempts at oppositional discourses struggle against their reduction to glamorous "media events," to the surfaces/textures/images of opposition rather than to its actuality as something that challenges the status quo.

Baudrillard sees the invasion of advertising into the social sphere as central in these sorts of change; taking over the public space, advertising, "no longer limited to its traditional language . . . organizes the architecture and realization of super objects." Adverts are our only architecture today, Baudrillard says, "great screens on which are reflected atoms, particles, molecules in motion. Not a public space or a true public space but gigantic spaces of circulation, ventilation and ephemeral connections."[8]

Much of what Baudrillard has to say about the absence of any

CONCLUSION

distinction between the private and the public space applies to MTV. This is yet one more distinction that postmodernism obliterates in its flattening out of things into a network or system, the parts all relying on each other. For Baudrillard, as we saw, the opposition between private and public has been effaced: "The one is no longer a spectacle, the other no longer a secret." The two have been submerged "in a sort of obscenity where the most intimate processes of our life become the virtual feeding ground of the media."

Some of the pleasures of the universe of communication mentioned by Baudrillard (no longer, he says, those of "manifestation, scenic and aesthetic, but rather of pure fascination, aleatory and psychotropic") are indeed those that MTV offers, and the flattening out of distinctions as we've seen puts the viewer in a kind of endless present not that dissimilar to the schizophrenic state. But I do not think we have yet arrived at Baudrillard's "cold universe." MTV rather signals a transitional period between the "hot" and the "cold" universes since, as noted, many videos still rely on Oedipal processes that belong to the old universe. Yet, on the other hand, MTV *does* manifest obliteration of the aesthetic distinctions that characterized the old, "hot" universe, and in this sense already looks toward the stage of the "ecstasy of communication" that Baudrillard envisages.

We cannot expect a commercial medium like MTV to resist the pressures of what may indeed be a deep cultural change. And as culture workers, we do not want to return to the error of insisting upon fixed points of enunciation labeled "truth"; but, as Tony Bennett and Ernesto Laclau have pointed out, we must continue to articulate oppositional discourses – recognizing them as discourses rather than an ontological truth that recent theory has cast doubt on – if we are to construct "new" subjects not totally defined by the reading formations of the postmodernist, "cold" universe. Important in this effort is more analysis of the televisual apparatus as it works to construct subjects unable any more to distinguish an "inside" from an "outside," "fiction" from "reality."

Afterword

Although writing this book on MTV has been an exciting experience, it has also been frustrating in various ways. There was first the difficulty of working in an area that was so new and had not been researched before; and second, of learning how to relate to the various managers, agencies, record companies, and the MTV management itself which became my only research sources and who were as unused to dealing with a cultural studies scholar like myself as I was to dealing with them. I have learned almost as much about MTV from my dealings with these institutions and their representatives as from anything I have ever read on the subject.

The lack of adequate research materials and particularly of any co-operation from MTV itself hampered my work. My only hope was to get the information from such sources, but this was where I often ran into problems. For example, trying to get dates for release of videos on MTV was difficult since MTV does not give out this information, for some unknown reason. I was forced to rely on the goodwill of people in the video departments of the various record companies, most of whom were pleasant and co-operative. However, I still could not verify release dates for every video, particularly for those made more than a year or so ago. There are as yet no reference books of any kind for MTV.

Another handicap was the sense of secrecy that surrounds a lot of the agents and managers, or their associates, whom one gets to speak to; I would confront a cagey, often wary voice on the other end of the line. People could not easily place me in a known category, often having as yet no experience with scholars writing about rock videos. Hence through nobody's fault I got shunted around a great deal, no-one seeming to know who could answer my questions about copyright, dates, permissions, etc. I often had the sense of dealing with vast interlocking networks, the parts of which did not always know about the others – a Kafkaesque experience of the whole organization being outside any one person's reach.

A different sort of frustration arose out of writing about something that was constantly changing. Even as I struggled to make generalizations, to codify, to formulate plausible theses and arguments, the channel would change and render a statement obsolete. In other words, the experience of writing the book was an experience of getting inside a postmodernist phenomenon. I was dealing with a body of material that would not stay the same, that was constantly transforming itself (like the image in Peter Gabriel's "Sledge-hammer") into something else even as I tried to grasp what it had just been. This phenomenon confirmed my sense of the relationship between constant transformation and the pressures of consumption that partly defines postmodernism.

This was most obvious in relation to the images of the stars that I was dealing with. In the past, with stars like Paul Anka, Elvis Presley, even the early Beatles or the Stones, the image that a star decided to promote remained relatively stable once a formula that produced commercial success had been found. If the image brought the fans out, and made them buy records and all the other star-paraphernalia, it would be exploited for a comparatively long time. But this is not the case with MTV stars who often undergo dramatic changes in the course of only months. For instance, Madonna, Pat Benatar, David Bowie, Prince, Tina Turner, Billy Idol, Motley Crue, to name only a few, have undergone major transformations over the past two years. Predictably, the stars making the more political videos (e.g. Bruce Springsteen, John Cougar Mellencamp, Tears for Fears), and who depend for their effect on a very personally committed and working-class appeal, on a stance in the world rather than on surfaces/textures/self-as-commodity, have not undergone such huge transformations.

155

One can only theorize about the increased rapidity of changes in star-images: it has partly to do with the increased exposure that stars get today compared with in the past – an increased exposure produced largely through television. It is the very mechanism of a 24-hour channel that creates the need for rapid image changes; the consumption value of the old image is quickly exhausted given the intensity of its circulation on a 24-hour channel. If we take twelve videos an hour as a reasonable average, then 228 videos are shown every 24 hours. If we multiply this by seven, we get 2016 videos shown a week. And if a star has a video being cycled at the high-density rate, his/her image could be on the channel (and in viewers' minds) every three or four hours. Obviously, how often any particular viewer gets to see the same image depends on frequency of watching, but the point is that there is a high rate of market saturation in the new situation – far higher than in earlier historical periods. The stars evidently feel a need to keep changing their images in order to keep up their consumption. Viewers quickly tire of the same image, given its high rate of circulation, and there is constant demand for something new.

The case of Billy Idol here is pertinent, and also exemplifies the kinds of frustration that I experienced in relation to getting permission to reprint images from videos discussed in my book. Idol's agent had from the start been unusually co-operative and also unusually interested in my project. He asked me to send him the entire manuscript, which I did; he also requested that I send copies of the precise images I wanted to use, which I also did. The agent was even encouraging about Idol's being willing to let me put one image on the cover of the book – something that I could not get anyone else to agree to. But when I called for written confirmation of verbal agreements, I was told in no uncertain terms that I could not use anything since Billy was in the middle of changing his image; he was bringing out a new record and did not want anything to do with his old image in circulation.

This sensitivity about the star's image was pervasive; one agent (trying to be helpful) warned me that one had to be very careful when dealing with stars' images: *I* might think I had chosen an attractive video frame, but the star might see it quite differently and think the image ugly. Many agents indicated that the star in question

AFTERWORD

refused to allow his/her image to be displayed in any way that he/
she could not completely control. Images on a book cover were evidently viewed with great suspicion as being precisely an example of
an image allowed to run wild, as it were. I was told that in the case of
a book cover the stars would not know where their image was being
displayed, and this they could not allow. An image on a book cover
also presumably "fixes" an image for too long which, as I've noted,
stars nowadays cannot afford.

I thus experienced firsthand what has been theorized about the
circulation of the image and its ties to consumption. In the case of
MTV, concerns take on a new dimension of urgency, since stars
believe that they must make constant changes to remain desirable. If
we look at the videos figuring Madonna in 1986, we can see extraordinarily rapid image changes. If the film *Desperately Seeking
Susan* (its video was called "Getting Into the Groove") brings to full
fruition an image Madonna had been working on in 1984–5, then
1986 reflected a series of efforts to abandon that image and replace
it with something else. There was first the suddenly suave, serious,
sleek image of the video "Live to Tell," again from a film; this was
followed by the further transformation of the image in "Papa Don't
Preach," where the figure is split between the Jean Seberg-style
bejeaned teenager and the slick, sexy woman in black. Finally, right
at the end of the year, a further dramatic change took place in the
video "Open Your Heart," although perhaps it was a development
of the sexy woman in "Papa Don't Preach." "Open Your Heart" is
a daring critique of "carousel" porn parlours, such as proliferate on
42nd Street. In the course of this critique, Madonna not only figures
as the girl inside the carousel who is being watched through windows
that encircle her (the voyeur pays a certain amount for a fixed length
of "seeing" time); but she also rescues an innocent young boy who
has wandered into the carousel and wants to "play" Madonna.
Madonna offers an uncharacteristic display of herself in traditional
porn costume (black corset, suspenders, black stockings, high-
heels, etc.), but at the end of the video, this sexy image is replaced by
a kind of androgynous one: Madonna decides not only to run away
from the parlor with the young boy, but to escape from sexuality
into innocent boyhood (she is seen dressed like the boy in old-
fashioned boy's clothes).

157

This sort of rapid change is increasingly demanded of the successful stars, whose images, just because of their success, quickly get saturated. As I tried to indicate throughout the book, the various types of videos that I outlined, from as early as 1982, also vary in popularity. For a few months the romantic seems to dominate, but then the nihilist type moves into the center; sometimes the socially conscious video (as in Summer 1986) comes to the fore, only to be followed by months when the postmodernist type becomes central. The one thing that has remained stable over the years studying MTV has been the five types I've outlined: the video technology has become more and more sophisticated, and production values for most of the videos now shown have gone up (videos are increasingly slick, professional, glossy, and using more and more elaborate, self-reflexive and deconstructive techniques), but the basic types remain the same. Perhaps, as I have tried to argue, the postmodernist aspects have begun increasingly to dominate videos of all types, but this has not yet reached a stage where the distinctions have become invalid (which I suppose could happen).

People often ask if I think that rock video and MTV are merely temporary phenomena which will be quickly exhausted. My sense is that the rock video is here to stay, although MTV as a 24-hour channel could change if competition from other such channels, or simply from the other sites of exhibition, increased so as to make their project unprofitable. It is possible that, like FM radio, TV channels could focus on one particular kind of rock video, or specialize in one type of rock/pop music. But so far there are no real signs to indicate this sort of change. For good or ill, MTV is most likely here to stay.

Any such change would emerge first from changes in what teenagers (and others MTV addresses) want from music video channels; and second from the receptivity of music television producers to changing audience tastes. As is clear from this book, I have not addressed myself to the level of historical viewers; I have been concerned with how MTV establishes itself as a production/consumption phenomenon rather than with how it is actually received by teenagers as historical subjects. MTV's postmodernist aspects may well be resisted or manipulated by such subjects in the viewing process. But research is needed to document this level of things. Theorizing the hypothetical or model spectator that a text constructs is compatible with studies of how historical spectators received texts. Different groups of teenagers no doubt use MTV in different ways according to class, race, and gender. However this may be, evidence of specific spectator behavior in no way invalidates the theory of MTV as a postmodernist form in its dominant modes of production, consumption, and exhibition.

Notes

INTRODUCTION

1 This figure was given to me by someone in the corporate office at Viacom.
2 Pittman is now President and Chief Executive Officer of MTV under Viacom.
3 Figures from unpublished paper by Gene Sobczak, "MTV, radio and unit sales," Rutgers University, June 1984, p. 12.
4 ibid.
5 *New York Times*, August 17, 1984, Section D.
6 ibid.
7 Cf. Sandy Flitterman, "The *real* soap operas: TV commercials," in E. Ann Kaplan, ed. *Regarding Television: Critical Approaches – An Anthology* (Los Angeles: American Film Institute, 1983), pp. 84-96.
8 Cf. Robert Stam, "Television news," in Kaplan (ed.), op. cit.
9 Margaret Phelan, "Panopticism and the uncanny: notes toward television's visual form," unpublished paper.
10 Cf. in particular *The Anti-Aesthetic: Essays on Postmodern Culture*, ed. Hal Foster (Port Townsend, Washington: The Bay Press, 1983).
11 There is already a quite formidable bibliography on the history of rock music. Perhaps the most solid sociological study remains Simon Frith's *The Sociology of Rock* (London: Constable, 1978), revised and updated in 1984. John Orman's recent *The Politics of Rock Music* (Chicago: Nelson-Hall, 1984) documents the subversive aspects of rock music in the 1960s, and the CIA's interest in rock stars, and ends up showing the increasing conservativism of rock stars and fans in the 1980s. John Eisen's uneven collection, *The Age of Rock: Sounds of*

NOTES

The American Cultural Revolution (New York: Random House, 1969) contains much discussion of rock's subversive aspects, while Nick Cohn's early *Rock From the Beginning* (New York: Stein & Day, 1969) takes a more cynical and skeptical stance.

12 Stuart Hall and Paddy Whannel, *The Popular Arts* (New York: Pantheon, 1965), especially chapter 2.

13 Cf. Stephen Melville, "Coda: The morning mail." Paper read at the Lacan Conference at The University of Amherst, Spring 1985. Some of this material has been incorporated into an article, "Psychoanalysis and the place of *jouissance*," *Critical Inquiry* (December 1986).

14 Greil Marcus, *Mystery Train: Images of America in Rock 'n' Roll Music* (New York: E.P. Dutton, 1975; rev. edn 1985).

15 Cohn, op. cit.; M. Jahn, *From Elvis Presley to the Rolling Stones* (New York: Quadrangle, 1973).

16 Students interested in the history of rock music should refer to the bibliography.

17 As of writing, there is a rich sub-culture of new rock sounds in major cities like New York. For reporting on the aficionado rock scene in New York, see Ron Cristgau's column in *The Village Voice*.

18 The exhibition presents what are seen as key examples of the rock video form. Titled "Music video: the industry and its fringes," the show has thirty videos by various artists. The form can be said to start with the Beatles' 1967 promos for "Penny Lane" and "Strawberry Fields," which exhibit the surrealist imitations so prevalent in current videos. Captain Beefheart's "Lick my Decals Off Baby," is already a classic, while Queen's "Bohemian Rapsody" was one of the first videos responsible for a song hit, and also prefigures MTV's interest in visual complexities. Cf. review by Jim Hoberman, *The Village Voice*, September 17, 1985, for more details.

1 MTV: ADVERTISING AND PRODUCTION

1 This is what Sandy Flitterman argues in "The *real* soap operas: TV commercials," in E. Ann Kaplan (ed.), *Regarding Television: Critical Approaches – An Anthology* (Los Angeles: American Film Institute, 1983), pp. 84-96.

2 Cf. the "Music Video Directors' Symposium," in *Variety*, Wednesday, March 14, 1985, especially p. 70, where Adam Friedman discusses how videos are becoming increasingly important to the record companies.

3 Cf. "Music Video Directors' Symposium," *Variety*, Wednesday, March 14, 1984.

4 Cf. Gene Sobczak, "MTV, radio and unit sales," Rutgers University, June 1984, p. 13.

5 "Music Video Directors' Symposium," op. cit., p. 70. Information was also obtained from an interview with New York Video Director, Eddie Barbarini.

6   John Rockwell early on suggested that this format would produce the most original results. Combining video with sound into something really new, he says, is the most innovative possibility. "Soon artists will begin to shape their aural imaginations to take account of the visual possibilities afforded them by the video medium, and will let the sounds in their heads affect the sights, abstract or realistic, that we see on the video screen." Cf. his "Rock is edging into video," *The New York Times*, July 29, 1979.

7   Ed Levine, "TV rocks with music," *The New York Times Magazine*, May 8, 1983, p. 43.

8   This material is taken from an interview with Dr York at a TV studio in New York, where Bob Lechterman and Eddie Barbarini were filming and directing (respectively) a video by the group "Petite" that Dr York was producing. Dr York indicated that one way for black artists to get accepted on American music channels like VH-1, MTV, U-68, or on the HBO and other slots on regular channels, was for them to have a record produced by a British record company. York believes the British market is far more open to black artists, and either has a large "quota" or no quota at all, as he thinks the American channels have.

9   Cf. discussions in popular articles, e.g. Steve Levy, "Ad nauseam – how MTV sells out rock and roll," *Rolling Stone*, December 8, 1983, pp. 36-7; comment by Arlene Zeichner in "Rock 'n Roll Video," *Film Comment*, vol. 19, no. 4 (July/August 1983), p. 45; Ron Gristgau, "Rock 'n roll coaster: the music biz on a joyride," *The Village Voice* (February 7, 1984), p. 43; Levine, op. cit: Levine notes here that Bob Pittman defends the few black bands by claiming that black and white pop music have always been separate – hardly any kind of justification for his practice!

10 The irony here, as Dr York pointed out, is that white musicians are using black forms in their rock; the Police and Sting play reggae, according to Dr York, while he characterized Wham!, Hall and Oates, and Madonna as playing "Blue-Eyed Soul."

11 Levy, op. cit, p. 33.

12 During 1986, there was a striking change in MTV logos: to begin with, the rocket logo was finally dropped altogether, ostensibly because of the Challenger disaster; but secondly, the logos now are immensely colorful, varied, and imaginative. There are animated, comic ones; abstract, patterned ones; the "MTV" letters are arranged in all imaginable ways that constantly engage one's attention. In addition, there are more direct ads for MTV in the form of interviews with people "on the street," saying what the channel means to them. It is as if the channel gave up trying to symbolize itself through the logos, and went instead for what would delight the eye.

13 Cf. Jane Feuer, "The concept of live television: ontology as ideology," in E. Ann Kaplan (ed.), *Regarding Television: Critical Approaches – An Anthology* (Los Angeles: American Film Institute, 1983), pp. 12-22.

NOTES

14 For an off-the-cuff look at the daily routine at MTV, including interviews with some of the Veejays and the pre-recording techniques, see Roberta Myers, "Behind the scenes at MTV," in *Careers*, Spring 1986, pp. 21-5.
15 The information reported here was gained by interviews with teenagers from The Bronx High School of Science, including Leo Margolf and Brett Kaplan, and from private schools including Paul Charney.
16 ibid.
17 Find below minute-by-minute outline of various MTV ad-segments (randomly chosen hours).

(a) ONE HOUR ON MTV: TAKEN FROM 5:22 TO 6:22, JUNE 25, 1985

5:22	Ad: Crazy Eddie (½)
	Ads: Announcement series: Hans Kleper Corp
	Copy Quick
	American Lung Association
	Manhattanville Records
5:24	MTV logo (Mystery Man) (seconds)
5:24	Video: Eurythmics, "There Must Be An Angel"
5:28	MTV spot (seconds)
5:28	Video: Elton John, "Act of War"
5:32	MTV spot (seconds)
5:32	Video: Duran Duran, "A View To Kill"
5:36	Video: Rod Stewart, "People Get Ready"
5:39	Goodman/Piscope interview
5:40	Ad: Three Musketeers
5:40	Ad: Jordache Jeans
5:41	Ad: Sun Country Wine Cooler
5:41	Bryan Adams: ad of own upcoming appearance
5:41	Interview Goodman/Piscope
5:45	Video: Katerina, "Walking on Sunshine"
5:48	
5:52	Goodman – commentary on Gina; notes Adams' upcoming appearance; notes the "Let's make a music deal" award
5:52	Ad for movie, *Back to the Future*
5:53	Milk ad
5:53	Juicy Fruit ad
5:54	Ad: Merry-Go-Round Fashions
5:54	Soft-Dri ad
5:55	MTV ad for all-American rock and roll weekend (military iconography)
5:55	Video: "I Drink Alone"
6:00	MTV logo: Men on Moon; Quinn's voice re what's coming up
6:01	Video: Cyndi Lauper's "Goonies"
6:06	Video: Julian Lennon, "Valotte"
6:10	Martha Quinn with concert tour info

6:12   Ad for Columbia Pictures movie *St Elmo's Fire*
6:12   Ad: shorts
6:13   Ad: Levis
6:15   Video: Ratt's "Lay It Down"
6:18   Video: Madonna, "Getting Into The Groove"
6:21   Quinn, announcing the countdown Friday at different times; also the music competition game
6:22   Ads: the announcement series that came on at 5:22

(b) HOUR RUNDOWN FROM 5:11 TO 6:11, JUNE 26, 1985

5:11   Film ad: *Back to the Future*
5:12   Ad for rock and roll weekend and Friday night countdown
5:13   Video: Hooters, "All You Zombies"
5:17   Video: Journey, "Send Her My Love"
5:21   Veejay (Goodman) advertising MTV "Black Satin Tour" jacket; telling us Benatar tape coming up
5:22   Ad for Institute of Technology
        Ad for Calvin Cooler drink
        Ad for American Heart Association
        Ad for Calvin Cooler
5:23   New York State Bar Association ad: anti-drink and drive
5:23   Announcement ad for Carrot Top Pastries
5:23   MTV logo
5:24   Video: Hall and Oates, "Possession/Obsession"
5:28   MTV logo
5:28   Tape Collins/Bailey interview followed by their video, "Easy Lover"
5:32   MTV logo
5:32   Video: Benatar, "Invincible"
5:36   Video: Pete Townshend, "Let My Love Open the Door"
5:39   Veejay (Goodman): send away for the music deal
5:39   Ad: Snickers Bar
5:40   Ad: for Musicland Record Store
5:41   Ad: for Golden Champagne
5:41   MTV music news re Sting, Scorpions, Motley Crue
5:42   Clip of Motley Crue talking about themselves
5:43   Video: Talking Heads, "Once in a Life Time"
5:48   Video: Duran Duran, "A View to a Kill"
5:51   Veejay (M. Quinn) music news
5:52   Ad for film, *Emerald Forest* (struggle of father to find the son)
5:53   Ad for Alberto Mousse
        Ad for Country Wine Cooler
5:54   Ad for Merry-Go-Round Clothes
        Ad for Carefree Gum
5:55   MTV ad

164

NOTES

5:59   MTV logo, Veejay (Quinn) voice over re the music competition
6:00   Video: Michael Jackson, "Beat It"
6:05   Veejay: music news
6:06   Power Slaties interview with veejay
6:07   Ad for milk
6:07   Ad for jeep
6:08   MTV ad re basement tapes competition (six new bands chosen)
6:09   Video: Robert Plant, "Little By Little"
6:13   Video: Chicago, "Along Came a Woman"

2   HISTORY, "READING FORMATIONS," AND THE TELEVISUAL APPARATUS IN MTV

1   Keith Tribe, "History and the production of memories," *Screen*, vol. 18, no. 4 (Winter 1977/8), p. 11.
2   ibid.
3   Cf. Emile Benveniste, *Problems of General Linguistics* (Miami: University of Miami Press, 1971).
4   Geoffrey Nowell-Smith, "A note on history/discourse" (Nowell-Smith's essay was a commentary on Metz's), *Edinburgh Magazine*, no. 1 (1976), p. 30.
5   Christian Metz, "History/discourse: a note on two voyeurisms," *Edinburgh Magazine*, no. 1 (1976), p. 24.
6   Foucault's *The Archaeology of Knowledge and the Discourse on Language*, trans. Alan Sheridan (New York: Pantheon, 1972) explicitly confronts the possibility of writing history. Foucault looks back on, and critiques, his own historical discourse in previous texts, while raising problems about the whole construction of academic disciplines themselves. A text like *The History of Sexuality, Volume I: An Introduction* (trans. Robert Hurley, New York: Random House, 1978), on the other hand, shows Foucault doing his kind of "history as discourse" work.
7   Foucault, op. cit., pp. 12-15.
8   Roland Barthes, "The death of the author," in *Image–Music–Text*, trans. Stephen Heath (New York: Hill & Wang, 1977), p. 148.
9   Metz, op. cit., p. 22.
10   David Morley, *The "Nationwide" Audience: Structure and Decoding*, BFI Television Monographs, no. 11 (London: British Film Institute, 1980).
11   Cf. Christine Gledhill, "Recent developments in feminist film criticism," *Quarterly Review of Film Studies*, vol. 3, no. 4 (1978), pp. 35-46. Reprinted in Mary Ann Doane, Pat Mellencamp, and Linda Williams, *Re-Vision: Essays in Feminist Film Criticism* (Los Angeles: American Film Institute, 1983), pp. 18-48.
12   Reprinted in Stephen Heath, *Questions of Cinema* (Bloomington, Ind.: Indiana University Press, 1981), pp. 113-30. Page numbers refer to this edition.

ROCKING AROUND THE CLOCK

13 Keith Tribe, op. cit.; and Janet Staiger, "Mass produced photoplays: economic and signifying practices in the first years of Hollywood," *Wide Angle*, vol. 4, no. 3 (1980), pp. 12-28. Cf. also David Bordwell, Kristin Thompson, and Janet Staiger, *The Classical Hollywood Film* (New York: Columbia University Press, 1985).

14 Cf. Ernesto Laclau, "Politics and the construction of the unthinkable," unpublished paper, cited by Bennett; and his "Populist rupture and discourse," *Screen Education*, no. 34 (Spring 1980); and Michel Pêcheux, *Language, Semantics and Ideology* (London: Macmillan, 1982).

15 Ron Levaco, "Eikenbaum, inner speech and film stylistics," *Screen*, vol. 15, no. 4 (Winter 1974/5), p. 48.

16 Tony Bennett, "Texts in history: the determinations of readings and their texts," in Derek Attridge, Geoffrey Bennington and Robert Young (eds), *Post-Structuralism and the Question of History* (Cambridge: Cambridge University Press, 1986).

17 Keith Tribe, op. cit., p. 12.

18 Mulvey, "Visual pleasure and narrative cinema," *Screen*, vol. 16, no 3 (Autumn 1975), pp. 6-18. This essay has been reprinted several times.

19 "Oedipus interruptus," *Wide Angle*, vol. 7, nos 1-2, pp. 34-41.

20 Robert Stam, "Television news and its spectator," in E. Ann Kaplan (ed.), *Regarding Television: Critical Approaches – An Anthology* (Los Angeles: American Film Institute, 1983), pp. 23-43. Cf. also what Sandy Flitterman-Lewis has to say on this topic in her essay "Fascination in Fragments: psychoanalysis in film and television," in Robert Allen (ed.) *Channels of Discourse: Television Criticism in the 80s* (Chapel Hill, NC: University of North Carolina Press, 1987).

21 Cf. Jane Feuer, "The concept of live television: ontology as ideology," in E. Ann Kaplan (ed.), op. cit., pp. 12-22; and Charlotte Brunsdon, "Crossroads: notes on soap opera," in E. Ann Kaplan (ed.), op. cit., pp. 76-82.

3 MTV AND THE AVANT-GARDE: THE EMERGENCE OF A POSTMODERNIST ANTI-AESTHETIC?

1 Cf. Diana Frampton, "Pop promo man moves into ads," *Broadcast*, August 2, 1985.

2 Jacques Lacan, "The mirror stage as formative of the function of the I," in his *Ecrits: A Selection*, trans. Alan Sheridan (New York and London: Norton, 1979), pp. 1-9.

3 Lacan, op. cit., especially pp. 56-76.

4 For more discussion of the implications for women of the Lacanian model, see Kaja Silverman, *The Subject of Semiotics* (New York: Oxford University Press, 1983), especially pp. 149-93. For further understanding of Lacan in general, see Anika Lemaire, *Jacques Lacan*, trans. David Macey (London: Routledge & Kegan Paul, 1977).

5   Cf. Roland Barthes, "Upon leaving the movie theatre," in Theresa Hak Kyung Cha (ed.), *Cinematic Apparatus: Selected Writings* (New York: Tanam Press, 1980), p. 3.

6   Cf. Jean Baudrillard, "The ecstasy of communication," in Hal Foster (ed.), *The Anti-Aesthetic: Essays in Postmodern Culture* (Port Townsend: Bay Press, 1983), pp. 126-33; and his essays in *Simulations*, trans. Paul Foss, Paul Patton, and Philip Beitchman (New York: Semiotext(e), 1983), especially pp. 30-48.

7   Cf. Rachel Bowlby, *Just Looking: Consumer Culture in Dreiser, Gissing and Zola* (London and New York: Methuen, 1985), especially pp. 1-17; and Peter Stallybrass and Allon White, *The Politics and Poetics of Transgression* (London and New York: Methuen/Cornell, 1986).

8   Fredric Jameson, "Postmodernism and consumer society," in Hal Foster (ed.), op. cit., pp. 111-25. Page numbers refer to this edition. A complete version of this essay appeared in *New Left Review* no. 146 (1984) as "Postmodernism, or The Cultural Logic of Late Capitalism".

9   Louis A. Sass, "Time, space and symbol: a study of narrative form and representational structure in madness and modernism," in *Psychoanalysis and Contemporary Thought*, vol. 8, no. 1 (1985), pp. 45-85.

4   IDEOLOGY, ADOLESCENT DESIRE, AND THE FIVE TYPES OF VIDEO ON MTV

1   Cf. Louis Althusser, "Ideology and ideological state apparatuses (notes towards an investigation)," in *Lenin and Philosophy and Other Essays*, trans. Ben Brewster (New York and London: Monthly Review Press, 1971), p. 180. Page numbers refer to this edition.

2   Jean Baudrillard, "The ecstasy of communication," in Hal Foster (ed.), *The Anti-Aesthetic: Essays in Postmodern Culture* (Port Townsend: Bay Press, 1983), p. 127.

3   For a full discussion of Baudrillard's ideas and their limitations, cf. André Frankovitz (ed.), *Seduced and Abandoned: The Baudrillard Scene* (New York and Glebe, Australia: Semiotext(e) and Stonemoss Services, 1984).

4   Cf. Jean Baudrillard, *Simulations*, trans. Paul Foss, Paul Patton, and Philip Beitchman (New York: Semiotext(e), 1983).

5   Lawrence Grossberg, "The politics of youth culture: some observations on rock and roll in American culture," *Social Text* (Winter 1983–4), pp. 110-11.

6   In a forthcoming book, *Motherhood and Representation*, I trace some of the history of mother images in film and literature – images that rock videos still draw upon.

7   Cf. Peter Stallybrass and Allon White, *The Politics and Poetics of Transgression* (London and New York: Methuen/Cornell, 1986), especially the introduction for a summary of Bakhtinian ideas of the carnival and of their critical uses, pp. 1-26.

8 Mikhail Bakhtin, *Rabelais and his World*, trans. H. Iswolsky (Cambridge, Mass.: MIT Press, 1968), p. 109. Quotes by Stallybrass and White, op. cit., p. 7.

9 Cf. discussion by Stallybrass and White, op. cit., p. 13.

10 As will be clear later on, videos by women stars are far fewer than those by male stars, and in the avant-garde category the imbalance is even greater. A recent series of programs of videos by female artists, going back to the 1970s, at Artists Space in New York (entitled "What does she want," and running from 2–27 November, 1985) demonstrated the range and creativity of much video work by women being done outside the mainstream. Laurie Anderson's creative "O Superman" was shown in that series; it is only because of her film *Home of the Brave* (given a short run at one New York theatre, The Bleecker Street Cinema) that her video made it to MTV.

11 John Orman, *The Politics of Rock Music* (Chicago: Nelson-Hall, 1984), pp. 164-5.

12 "He's on fire: America's latest rock-and-roll hero has the fans going wild about the boss," *Newsweek*, August 15, 1985, pp. 4-9.

13 Cf. Jean Baudrillard, *In the Shadow of the Silent Majorities . . . Or the End of the Social and Other Essays*, trans. Paul Foss, Paul Patton, and John Johnston (New York: Semiotext(e), 1983), p. 26. Page numbers refer to this edition.

5 GENDER ADDRESS AND THE GAZE IN MTV

1 For recent discussion of differences between the filmic and televisual apparatus cf. Sandy Flitterman-Lewis, "Fascination in Fragments: psychoanalysis in film and television," in Robert Allen (ed.) *Channels of Discourse: Television Criticism in the 80s* (Chapel Hill, NC: University of North Carolina Press, 1987).

2 Cf. summaries of recent feminist work, together with bibliographies in Annette Kuhn, *Women's Pictures: Feminism and Cinema* (London: Routledge & Kegan Paul, 1982): E. Ann Kaplan, *Women and Film: Both Sides of the Camera* (London and New York: Methuen, 1983); P. Mellencamp, Mary Ann Doane, and Linda Williams (eds), *Re-Vision: Essays in Feminist Film Criticism* (Los Angeles: American Film Institute, 1984).

3 Cf., for example, Teresa de Lauretis, *Alice Doesn't: Feminism, Cinema, and Semiotics* (Bloomington, Indiana: Indiana University Press, 1984); or Gaylyn Studlar, "Masochism and the perverse pleasures of cinema," in Bill Nichols (ed.), *Movies and Methods*, vol. II (Berkeley and Los Angeles: University of California Press, 1985), pp. 602-24.

4 Mary Ann Doane, "Woman's stake: filming the female body," *October*, no. 17 (1981), pp. 29-30.

5 Discussion of the episode is in Sigmund Freud, *Beyond the Pleasure Principle*, Standard Edition, XVIII, pp. 14-17.

NOTES

6   Cf. Daniel Stern, "Mother and infant at play: the dyadic interaction involving facial, vocal and gaze behaviors," in M. Lewis and L.A. Rosenblaum (eds), *The Origins of Behavior*: vol. 1, *The Effect of the Infant on the Caregiver* (New York: Wiley, 1974). And Selma Fraiberg, *Every Child's Birthright: In Defense of Mothering* (New York: Basic Books, 1977).
7   In her more usual vein, Pat Benatar early on anticipated the recent "tough woman" look of many female vocalists. In 1981, Nick Wright quoted her as saying "I hardly ever listen to other female vocalists. It's the British male rock stars I admire most. . . . Low-keyed and laid back I'm not. A lot of women singers today seem to be saying 'If you love me and then hurt me, I'll die.' I say, 'If you love me and then hurt me, I'll kick your ass.'" Nick Wright, "Pat Benatar," in *The Year in Rock, 1981-82*, ed. John Swenson (New York: Delilah Books, Putnam, 1981), p. 16.
8   Quoted by Stephen Holden in "The pop life: a spicy new album by Carly Simon," *The New York Times*, Wednesday, August 7, 1985, C16.
9   Cf. Stephen Holden, "Review of Paul Young," *The New York Times*, Wednesday, August 7, 1985.
10 Cf. Deborah Frost, "White noise: how heavy metal rules," *The Village Voice*, vol. XXX, no. 25 (June 18, 1985), pp. 46-9.
11 Cf. David Fricke, "Heavy metal," in *The Year in Rock*, op. cit. According to Fricke, the Sex Pistols "embodied the seething anger and snow-balling frustration of British youth faced with rising unemployment and a dead-end economy." Fricke goes on to note that "the recent riots in England, are, for the most part, Johnny Rotten's prophecy come true" (p. 20).
12 Cf. E. Ann Kaplan, "Pornography and/as representation," forthcoming in *Enclitic*; cf. also the Brief by Sally Law and Nan Hunter written for the Indianapolis Lawsuit about Censorship of Pornography.
13 Cf. Jane D. Brown and Kenneth C. Campbell, "Race and gender in music videos: The same beat but a different drummer," *Journal of Communication*, vol. 36, no. 1 (winter 1986), pp. 94-107.

6   CONCLUSION: MTV, POSTMODERNISM, AND THE TELEVISUAL APPARATUS

1   See notes to Introduction for relevant citations.
2   Fredric Jameson, "Postmodernism and consumer society," in Hal Foster (ed.), *The Anti-Aesthetic: Essays in Postmodern Culture* (Port Townsend: Bay Press, 1983), p. 116.
3   ibid., p. 119.
4   ibid., p. 119.
5   ibid., p. 120.
6   ibid., p. 121.
7   Lawrence Grossberg, "The politics of youth culture: some observations

on rock and roll in American culture," *Social Text* (Winter 1983-4), p. 111.

8 Jean Baudrillard, "The ecstasy of communication," in Hal Foster (ed.), op. cit.

Videography

(Videos mentioned in the book)

AC/DC
"For Those About to Rock We Salute You"
For Those About to Rock
Atlantic Records, 1985

AC/DC
"Who Made Who"
Maximum Overdrive
Motion Picture Soundtrack
Atlantic Records, 1986
DeLaurentiis Entertainment Corp.

Bryan Adams
"Heaven"
Reckless
A & M Records, 1985

a—ha
"Take On Me"
Hunting High and Low
Warner Bros Records, 1984
Director: Steve Barron

a—ha
"Train of Thought"
Hunting High and Low
Warner Bros Records, 1985

Laurie Anderson
"Language Is A Virus"
Home of the Brave
Motion Picture Soundtrack
Warner Bros Records, 1986

The Art of Noise
"Paranoimia"
Invisible Silence
Chrysalis Records, 1986

Artists Against Apartheid
"Sun-City"
Manhattan Records, 1986

Asia
"Only Time Will Tell"
Asia
Geffen Records, 1983

Philip Bailey and Phil Collins
"Easy Lover"
Chinese Wall
Columbia/CBS Records, 1986

Bangles
"Manic Monday"
Different Light
Columbia/CBS Records, 1986

ROCKING AROUND THE CLOCK

Jimmy Barnes
"Working Class Man"
Gung Ho
Motion Picture Soundtrack
Geffen Records/Paramount
Pictures, 1986

Pat Benatar
"Love is a Battlefield"
Get Nervous
Chrysalis Records, 1983

Pat Benatar
"Sex as a Weapon"
Seven The Hard Way
Chrysalis Records, 1986

Pat Benatar
"We Belong"
Tropico
Chrysalis Records, 1984

David Bowie
"DJ"
The Lodge
RCA Records, 1983

David Bowie
"Modern Love"
Let's Dance
EMI/America Records, 1984

David Bowie
"China Girl"
Let's Dance
EMI/America Records, 1984

David Bowie
"Blue Jean"
Tonight
EMI/America Records, 1984

David Bowie
"Absolute Beginners"
Absolute Beginners
Motion Picture Soundtrack
EMI/America Records/Orion
Pictures, 1986
Director: Julian Temple

David Bowie and Mick Jagger
"Dancing In The Street"
EMI/America Records, 1985

Jackson Brown
"For America"
Lives In The Balance
Elektra/Asylum Records, 1986

Julie Brown
"The Homecoming Queen's Got a
Gun"
Goddess In Progress
Rhino Records, 1984

Kim Carnes
"Bette Davis' Eyes"
Mistaken Identity
EMI/America Records, 1984

Cars
"You Might Think"
Heartbeat City
Elektra Records, 1984

Cars
"Why Can't I Have You"
Heartbeat City
Elektra Records, 1985

Phil Collins
"One More Night"
No Jacket Required
Atlantic Records, 1985

Phil Collins
"Don't Lose My Number"
No Jacket Required
Atlantic Records, 1985

John Cougar Mellencamp
"Authority Song"
Uh—Huh
Riva/Polygram Records, 1984

John Cougar Mellencamp
"ROCK In The USA"
Scarecrow
Riva/Polygram Records, 1986

VIDEOGRAPHY

John Cougar Mellencamp
"Lonely Ol' Night"
Scarecrow
Riva/Polygram Records, 1985

John Cougar Mellencamp
"Small Town"
Scarecrow
Riva/Polygram Records, 1985

John Cougar Mellencamp
"Hurts So Good"
American Fool
Riva/Polygram Records, 1982

John Cougar Mellencamp
"Rain on the Scarecrow"
Scarecrow
Riva/Polygram Records, 1986

Motley Crue
"Smokin' in the Boys' Room"
Theatre of Pain
Elektra Records, 1985

Motley Crue
"Home Sweet Home"
Theatre of Pain
Elektra Records, 1985

Dire Straits
"Money for Nothing"
Brothers in Arms
Warner Bros Records, 1985
Director: Steve Barron

Dire Straits
"So Far Away"
Brothers In Arms
Warner Bros Records, 1985

Dire Straits
"Walk of Life"
Brothers in Arms
Warner Bros Records, 1986

Dokken
"Alone Again"
Tooth and Nail
Elektra Records, 1985

The Dream Academy
"Life in a Northern Town"
The Dream Academy
Warner Bros Records, 1986

Duran Duran
"Reflex"
Seven and The Ragged Tiger
Capitol Records, 1983

Duran Duran
"Rio"
Rio
Capitol Records, 1983

Duran Duran
"A View to a Kill"
Original Motion Picture Soundtrack
Capitol Records, 1985

Duran Duran
"Wild Boys"
Arena
Capitol Records, 1985

ELO
"Calling America"
Balance of Power
CBS/Associated Records, 1985

Eurythmics
"Here Comes the Rain Again"
Be Yourself Tonight
RCA Records, 1984

Eurythmics
"Would I Lie to You?"
Be Yourself Tonight
RCA Records, 1985

Eurythmics
"There Must Be An Angel
(Playing With My Heart)"
Be Yourself Tonight
RCA Records, 1985

Eurythmics
"Sexcrime
1984 (For the Love of the Big Brother)
RCA Records, 1984

173

Eurythmics
"Missionary Man"
Revenge
RCA Records, 1986

Fabulous Thunderbirds
"Tuff Enuff"
Tuff Enuff
CBS Associated Records, 1986

Falco
"Rock Me Amadeus"
Falco 3
A & M Records, 1986

The Firm
"Radioactive"
The Firm
Atlantic Records, 1985

The Firm
"Live In Peace"
Mean Business
Atlantic Records, 1986

John Fogerty
"The Old Man Down The Road"
Centerfield
Warner Bros Records, 1984

John Fogerty
"Rock and Roll Girls"
Centerfield
Warner Bros Records, 1984

Foreigner
"I Want To Know What Love Is"
Agent Provocateur
Atlantic Records, 1984

Frankie Goes to Hollywood
"Relax"
Welcome To The Pleasure Dome
ZTT/Island Records, 1983

Frankie Goes to Hollywood
"Two Tribes"
Welcome To The Pleasure Dome
ZTT/Island Records, 1984

Frankie Goes to Hollywood
"Welcome to the Pleasure Dome"
Welcome To The Pleasure Dome
ZTT/Island Records, 1985

Aretha Franklin
"Freeway of Love"
Who's Zoomin' Who?
Arista Records, 1985

Aretha Franklin
"Another Night"
Who's Zoomin' Who?
Arista Records, 1986

Aretha Franklin and Annie Lennox
"Sisters Are Doin' It For
Themselves"
Be Yourself Tonight
RCA Records, 1986

Glen Frey
"Smuggler's Blues"
The Allnighter
MCA Records, 1985

Glen Frey
"You Belong to the City"
Miami Vice Soundtrack
MCA Records, 1986

Glen Frey
"The Heat Is On"
Beverly Hills Cop
Motion Picture Soundtrack
MCA Records, 1985

Peter Gabriel
"Shock the Monkey"
Peter Gabriel
Geffen Records, 1985

Peter Gabriel
"Sledgehammer"
So
Geffen Records, 1986

Genesis
"Invisible Touch"
Invisible Touch
Atlantic Records, 1986

174

VIDEOGRAPHY

Sammy Hagar
"VOA"
VOA
Geffen Records, 1985

Sammy Hagar
"I Can't Drive at 55"
VOA
Geffen Records, 1985

Van Halen
"Jump"
1984
Warner Bros Records, 1983

Van Halen
"Hot for Teacher"
1984
Warner Bros Records, 1984

Daryl Hall
"Dreamtime"
The Three In The Happy Machine
RCA Records, 1986

Daryl Hall and John Oats
"Out of Touch"
Big Bam Boom
RCA Records, 1984

Daryl Hall and John Oates (with
David Ruffin and Eddie Kendrick)
"Live At The Apollo"
RCA Records, 1985

Heart
"What About Love"
Heart
Capitol Records, 1985

Heart
"Nothin' At All"
Heart
Capitol Records, 1986
Director: Milton Lage

Heart
"These Dreams"
Heart
Capitol Records, 1986

Don Henley
"Boys of Summer"
Building the Perfect Beast
Geffen Records, 1984

Don Henley
"All She Wants to do is Dance"
Building the Perfect Beast
Geffen Records, 1985

Honeymoon Suite
"Feel It Again"
The Big Prize
(Used Digital Disk)
Warner Bros Records, 1986
Director: Danny Kleinman

Whitney Houston
"How Will I Know"
Whitney Houston
Arista Records, 1985

Whitney Houston
"Greatest Love of All"
Whitney Houston
Arista Records, 1986

Billy Idol
"Rebel Yell"
Rebel Yell
Chrysalis Records, 1983

Billy Idol
"White Wedding"
Billy Idol
Chrysalis Records, 1986

INXS
"What You Need"
Listen Like Thieves
Atlantic Records, 1986

Janet Jackson
"What Have You Done For Me
Lately"
Control
A & M Records, 1986

175

ROCKING AROUND THE CLOCK

Jermaine Jackson
"I Think It's Love"
Precious Moment
Arista Records, 1986

Michael Jackson
"Thriller"
Thriller
Epic/CBS Records, 1983

Michael Jackson
"Beat It"
Thriller
Epic/CBS Records, 1984

Michael Jackson
"Billy Jean"
Thriller
Epic/CBS Records, 1984
Director: Steve Barron

The Rolling Stones
"She Was Hot"
Under Cover
CBS Records, 1983

Mick Jagger
"Harlem Shuffle"
Dirty Work
Rolling Stones Records, 1986

Mick Jagger and David Bowie
"Dancing In The Street"
EMI/America Records, 1985

Mick Jagger and Bette Midler
"Beast of Burden"
No Frills
Atlantic Records, 1984

Elton John
"That's Why They Call It The Blues"
Too Low for Zero
Geffen Records, 1984

Elton John
"Heartache All Over"
Leather Jackets
Geffen Records, 1986

Grace Jones
"Love Is The Drug"
Island Life
Island Records, 1986

Judas Priest
"Locked In"
Turbo
Columbia Records, 1986

Kiss
"The Tears Are Falling"
Asylum
Mercury/Polygram Records, 1986

Cyndi Lauper
"Time After Time"
She's So Unusual
Portrait Records, 1983

Cyndi Lauper
"Money Changes Everything"
She's So Unusual
Portrait Records, 1984

Cyndi Lauper
"Girls Just Want to Have Fun"
She's So Unusual
Portrait Records, 1983

Julian Lennon
"Stick Around"
The Secret Value of Daydreams
Atlantic Records, 1986

Annie Lennox and Aretha Franklin
"Sisters Are Doin' It For
Themselves"
Be Yourself Tonight
RCA Records, 1986

Madonna
"Lucky Star"
Madonna
Sire/Warner Bros Records, 1984

Madonna
"Borderline"
Madonna
Sire/Warner Bros Records, 1984

VIDEOGRAPHY

Madonna
"Like a Virgin"
Like a Virgin
Warner Bros Records, 1984

Madonna
"Getting Into The Groove"
Desperately Seeking Susan
Motion Picture Soundtrack
Orion Pictures, 1985
Producer: Stephen Ray

Madonna
"Material Girl"
Madonna
Sire/Warner Bros Records, 1985

Madonna
"Live To Tell"
At Close Range
Motion Picture Soundtrack
Hemdale Film/Orion Pictures, 1986

Madonna
"Papa Don't Preach"
True Blue
Sire/Warner Bros Records, 1986

Mama's Boys
"Mama, We're All Crazy Now"
Mama's Boys
Sire/Arista Records, 1984

Bette Midler and Mick Jagger
"Beast of Burden"
No Frills
Atlantic Records, 1984

Midnight Oil
"Best of Both Worlds"
Red Sails In The Sunset
Columbia/CBS Records, 1985

Ozzy Osbourne
"Shot in the Dark"
The Ultimate Sin
CBS Associated Records, 1986

Robert Palmer
"Addicted to Love"
Riptide
Island Records, 1985

Robert Palmer
"I Didn't Mean To Turn You On"
Riptide
Island Records, 1986

John Parr
"Naughty Naughty"
John Parr
Atlantic Records, 1984

Tom Petty and the Heartbreakers
"Don't Come Around Here No More"
Southern Accents
MCA Records, 1985

Pointer Sisters
"Neutron Dance"
Beverly Hills Cop
Motion Picture Soundtrack
Paramount Pictures/MCA Records, 1985

Police
"Synchronicity"
Synchronicity Concert
Home Video
A & M Home Video/IRS Video, 1985

The Powerstation
"Some Like It Hot"
Some Like It Hot
Capitol Records, 1985

Prince
"1999"
1999
Warner Bros Records, 1985

Prince
"Raspberry Beret"
Around the World in a Day
Paisley Park/Warner Bros Records, 1985

Prince
"Kiss"
Parade
Under the Cherry Moon

Motion Picture Soundtrack
Paisley Park/Warner Bros
Records, 1986

Queen
"Radio Ga Ga"
The Works
Capitol Records, 1983

Queen
"Princes of the Universe"
The Highland Album
Capitol Records, 1986

Lionel Ritchie
"Hello"
Can't Slow Down
Motown Records, 1984

Lionel Ritchie
"Dancing on the Ceiling"
Dancing on the Ceiling
Motown Records, 1986

Romantics
"Talking in Your Sleep"
In Heat
Nemperor/CBS Records, 1983

David Lee Roth
"California Girls"
Crazy From The Heat
Warner Bros Records, 1985

David Lee Roth
"Just Like a Gigolo (I Ain't Got
Nobody)"
Crazy From the Heat
Warner Bros Records, 1985

David Lee Roth
"Yankie Rose"
Eat 'Em And Smile
Warner Bros Records, 1986

David Lee Roth
"Going Crazy
Eat 'Em And Smile
Warner Bros Records, 1986

Run–DMC
"Walk This Way"
Raising Hell
Profile Records, 1986

Scorpions
"Rock You Like a Hurrican"
Love At First Sting
Mercury/Polygram Records, 1984

Scorpions
"Big City Nights"
World Wide Live
Mercury/Polygram Records, 1985

Scorpions
"No One Like You"
World Wide Live
Mercury/Polygram Records, 1986

Bob Seger and The Silver Bullet
Band
"Old Time Rock and Roll"
Stranger In Town
From the Movie *Risky Business*
Capitol Records, 1983

Simple Minds
"Don't You Forget About Me"
The Breakfast Club
Motion Picture Soundtrack
A & M Records, 1985

Simple Minds (with Robin Clark)
"Alive and Kicking"
Once Upon A Time
A & M Records, 1985
Director: Zybigniew Rybczynski

Simple Minds (with Robin Clark)
"All The Things She Said"
Once Upon A Time
Digital Disk Video
A & M Records, 1986
Director: Zybigniew Rybczynski

Sly Fox
"Let's Go All The Way"
Sly Fox
Capitol Records, 1986

VIDEOGRAPHY

Bruce Springsteen
"Born in the USA"
Born in the USA
Columbia/CBS Records, 1984
Director: John Sayles

Bruce Springsteen
"Dancing in the Dark"
Born in The USA
Columbia/CBS Records, 1984

Bruce Springsteen
"I'm On Fire"
Born in The USA
Columbia/CBS Records, 1985

Bruce Springsteen
"Glory Days"
Born in the USA
Columbia/CBS Records, 1985

Rod Stewart
"Infatuation"
Camouflage
Warner Bros Records, 1984

Rod Stewart
"Baby Jane"
Body Wishes
Warner Bros Records, 1985

Sting
"Fortress Around Your Heart"
The Dream of the Blue Turtles
A & M Records, 1985

Sting
"If You Love Somebody, Set
Them Free"
The Dream of the Blue Turtles
A & M Records, 1985

Donna Summer
"She Works Hard for the Money"
She Works Hard For The Money
Mercury/Polygram Records, 1983

Talking Heads
"Burning Down The House"
Speaking In Tongues
Sire/Warner Bros Records, 1986

Talking Heads
"Road To Nowhere"
Speaking In Tongues
Sire/Warner Bros Records, 1986

Tears For Fears
"Shout"
The Hunting
Mercury/Polygram Records, 1985

Tears For Fears
"Mother's Talk"
Songs From The Big Chair
Mercury/Polygram Records, 1986

Tina Turner
"What's Love Got To Do With It?"
Private Dancer
Capitol Records, 1984

Tina Turner
"Private Dancer"
Private Dancer
Capitol Records, 1984

Tina Turner
"Typical Male"
Break Every Rule
Capitol Records, 1986

Twisted Sister
"Leader of the Pack"
Come Out And Play
Atlantic Records/Atlantic Video,
1985

USA For Africa
"We Are The World"
USA For Africa
Columbia/CBS Records, 1985

Gino Vannelli
"Black Cars"
Black Cars
HME/CBS Records, 1985

Weird Al
"Like A Surgeon"
Dare To Be Stupid
Rock—N—Roll/CBS Records, 1985

Wham!
"Freedom"
Make It Big
Columbia/CBS Records, 1985

Wham!
"Bad Boys"
Make It Big
Columbia/CBS Records, 1984

Paul Young
"Everytime You Go Away"
The Secret of Association
Columbia/CBS Records, 1985

ZZ Top
"Legs Illuminator"
Illuminator
Warner Bros Records, 1984

ZZ Top
"Rough Boy"
Afterburner
Warner Bros Records, 1986
Director: Steve Barron

Y & T
"Summer Time Girl"
Open Fire
A & M Records, 1986

Bibliography

Althusser, Louis, "Ideology and ideological state apparatuses (notes towards an investigation)," in *Lenin and Philosophy and Other Essays*, trans. Ben Brewster (New York and London: Monthly Review Press, 1971), pp. 127–86.

Barthes, Roland, *Image–Music–Text*, trans. Stephen Heath (New York: Hill & Wang, 1977).

Barthes, Roland, "Upon leaving the movie theatre," in Theresa Hak Kyung Cha, ed., *Cinematic Apparatus: Selected Writings* (New York: Tanam Press, 1980), pp. 3–10.

Baudrillard, Jean, *Simulations*, trans. Paul Foss, Paul Patton, and Philip Beitchman (New York: Semiotext(e), 1983).

Baudrillard, Jean, *In the Shadow of the Silent Majorities . . . Or The End of the Social And Other Essays*, trans. Paul Foss, Paul Patton, and John Johnston (New York: Semiotext(e), 1983).

Baudrillard, Jean, "The ecstasy of communication," in Hal Foster, ed., *The Anti-Aesthetic: Essays in Postmodern Culture* (Port Townsend: Bay Press, 1983), pp. 125–36.

Bennett, Tony, "Texts in history: the determinations of readings and their texts," in Derek Attridge, Geoffrey Bennington, and Robert Young, eds, *Post-Structuralism and the Question of History* (Cambridge: Cambridge University Press, 1986).

Benveniste, Emile, *Problems of General Linguistics* (Miami, Fla: University of Miami Press, 1971).

Bordwell, David, Thompson, Kristin, and Staiger, Janet, *The Classical Hollywood Film* (New York: Columbia University Press, 1985).

Bowlby, Rachel, *Just Looking: Consumer Culture in Dreiser, Gissing and Zola* (London and New York: Methuen, 1985).

181

Brown, Jane D., and Campbell, Kenneth C., "Race and gender in music videos: the same beat but a different drummer," *Journal of Communication*, vol. 36, no. 1 (Winter 1986), pp. 94–106.

Brunsdon, Charlotte, "Crossroads: Notes on Soap Opera", in E. Ann Kaplan, ed., *Regarding Television: Critical Approaches – An Anthology* (Los Angeles: American Film Institute, 1983), pp. 76–82.

Chen, Kuan-Hsing, "MTV: the (dis)appearance of postmodern semiosis, or the cultural politics of resistance," *Journal of Communication Inquiry*, vol. 10, no. 1 (Winter 1986), pp. 66–9.

Cohn, Nick, *Rock From the Beginning* (New York: Stein & Day, 1969).

De Lauretis, Teresa, "Oedipus interruptus," *Wide Angle*, vol. 7, nos 1–2 (1986), pp. 34–41. Cf. her extended discussion of similar issues in her *Alice Doesn't: Feminism, Cinema and Semiotics* (Bloomington, Indiana: Indiana University Press, 1984).

Doane, Mary Ann, "Woman's stake: filming the female body," *October*, no. 17 (1981), pp. 23–36.

Eisen, John, ed., *The Age of Rock: Sounds of the American Cultural Revolution* (New York: Random House, 1969).

Feuer, Jane, "The concept of live television: ontology as ideology," in E. Ann Kaplan, ed., *Regarding Television: Critical Approaches – An Anthology* (Los Angeles: American Film Institute, 1983), pp. 12–22.

Fiske, John, "MTV: post structural post modern," *Journal of Communication Inquiry*, vol. 10, no. 1 (Winter 1986), pp. 74–9.

Flitterman-Lewis, Sandy, "The *real* soap operas: TV commercials," in E. Ann Kaplan, ed., *Regarding Television: Critical Approaches – An Anthology* (Los Angeles: American Film Institute, 1983), pp. 84–96.

Flitterman-Lewis, Sandy, "Fascination in fragments: psychoanalysis in film and television," in Robert Allen, ed., *Channels of Discourse: Television and Contemporary Criticism* (Chapel Hill: University of North Carolina Press, 1987).

Foster, Hal, ed., *The Anti-Aesthetic: Essays in Postmodern Culture* (Port Townsend, Washington: Bay Press, 1983).

Foucault, Michel, *The Archaeology of Knowledge and The Discourse on Language*, trans. Alan Sheridan (New York: Pantheon, 1972).

Fraiberg, Selma, *Every Child's Birthright: In Defense of Mothering* (New York: Basic Books, 1977).

Frankovitz, André, ed., *Seduced and Abandoned: The Baudrillard Scene* (New York and Glebe, Australia: Semiotext(e) and Stonemoss Services, 1984).

Freud, Sigmund, *Beyond the Pleasure Principle*, Standard Edition, vol. XVIII, pp. 14–17.

Freud, Sigmund, "Female sexuality," in James Strachey, ed., *Collected Papers*, vol. 5 (New York: Basic Books, 1959), pp. 252–72.

Fricke, David, "Heavy metal," in John Swenson, ed., *The Year in Rock, 1981–82* (New York: Putnam, 1981), pp. 16ff.

Frith, Simon, *The Sociology of Rock* (London: Constable, 1978; revised and updated 1984).

BIBLIOGRAPHY

Frost, Deborah, "White noise: how heavy metal rules," *The Village Voice*, vol. XXX, no. 25 (18 June 1985), pp. 46–9.

Gledhill, Christine, "Recent developments in feminist film criticism," *Quarterly Review of Film Studies*, vol. 3, no. 4 (1978), pp. 35–46; revised and reprinted in Mary Ann Doane, Patricia Mellencamp, and Linda Williams, eds, *Re-Vision: Essays in Feminist Film Criticism* (Los Angeles: American Film Institute, 1983), pp. 18–48.

Grossberg, Lawrence, "The politics of youth culture: some observations on rock and roll in American culture," *Social Text* (Winter 1983–4), pp. 107–14.

Hall, Stuart, and Whannel, Paddy, *The Popular Arts* (New York: Pantheon 1965).

Heath, Stephen, *Questions of Cinema* (Bloomington, Ind.: Indiana University Press, 1981).

Hoberman, Jim, "Music video: the industry and its fringes," review of Museum of Modern Art exhibition, *The Village Voice*, 17 September 1985.

Holdstein, D., "Music video: messages and structures," *Jump Cut*, no. 29 (1984), pp. 1, 6.

Jahn, M., *From Elvis Presley to the Rolling Stones* (New York: Quadrangle, 1973).

Jameson, Fredric, "Postmodernism and consumer society," in Hal Foster, ed., *The Anti-Aesthetic: Essays in Postmodern Culture* (Port Townsend: Bay Press, 1983), pp. 111–25.

Jameson, Fredric, *The Political Unconscious* (Ithaca, NY: Cornell University Press, 1981).

Journal of Communication Inquiry, vol. 10, no. 1 (Winter 1986). Entire issue devoted to essays on MTV.

Journal of Communication vol. 36, no. 1 (Winter 1986). Cf. focus on essays about music television in this issue.

Kaplan, E. Ann, *Women and Film: Both Sides of the Camera* (London and New York: Methuen, 1983).

Kaplan, E. Ann, ed., *Regarding Television: Critical Approaches – An Anthology* (Los Angeles: American Film Institute, 1983).

Kaplan, E. Ann, "A postmodern play of the signifier? Advertising, pastiche and schizophrenia in music television," in Philip Drummond and Richard Paterson, eds, *Television in Transition* (London: British Film Institute, 1985), pp. 146–63.

Kaplan, E. Ann, "History, the historical spectator and gender address in music television," *Journal of Communication Inquiry*, vol. 10, no. 1 (Winter 1986), pp. 3–14.

Kaplan, E. Ann, "Sexual difference, visual pleasure and the construction of the spectator in music television," *The Oxford Literary Review*, vol. 8, nos 1–2 (1986), pp. 113–22.

Kaplan, E. Ann, "Feminist film criticism: current issues and problems," *Studies in the Literary Imagination*, vol. XIX, no. 1 (Spring 1986), pp. 7–20.

ROCKING AROUND THE CLOCK

Kaplan, E. Ann, *Motherhood and Representation: The Maternal Discourse in Popular Literature and Film, 1830 to the Present* (London and New York: Methuen, forthcoming).

Kaplan, E. Ann, "Feminist criticism in television studies," in Robert Allen, ed., *Channels of Discourse: Television and Contemporary Criticism* Chapel Hill: University of North Carolina Press, 1986).

Kaplan, E. Ann, "Whose imaginary? Text, body and narrative in select rock videos," in Deidre Pribram, ed., *Cinematic Pleasure and the Female Spectator* (London: Verso, 1987).

Kaplan, E. Ann, and Phelan, Margaret, *The Fascination of Music Television: An Anthology.* (Forthcoming).

Kinder, Marsha, "Music video and the spectator: television, ideology and the dream," *Film Quarterly*, vol. 38, no. 1 (1985), pp. 1–15.

Lacan, Jacques, *Écrits: A Selection*, trans. Alan Sheridan (New York: Norton, 1979).

Laclau, Ernesto, "Populist rupture and discourse," *Screen Education*, no. 34 (Spring 1980).

Levaco, Ron, "Eikenbaum, inner speech and film stylistics," *Screen*, vol. 15, no. 4 (Winter 1974–5), pp. 47–58.

Levy, Stephen, "Ad nauseam – how MTV sells out rock and roll," *Rolling Stone*, 8 December 1983, pp. 36–9.

Marcus, Greil, *Mystery Train: Images of America in Rock 'n Roll Music* (New York: Dutton, 1975; rev. edn 1985).

Melville, Stephen, "Coda: the morning mail," paper delivered at the Lacan Conference, University of Amherst, Spring 1985. Much of the paper is included in "Psychoanalysis and the place of *jouissance*," *Critical Inquiry* (December 1986).

Metz, Christian, *Film Language: A Semiotics of the Cinema*, trans. Michael Taylor (New York: Oxford University Press, 1974).

Metz, Christian, "History/discourse: a note on two voyeurisms," *Edinburgh Magazine*, no. 1 (1976), pp. 21–5.

Morley, David, *The "Nationwide" Audience: Structure and Decoding*, BFI Television Monographs, no. 11 (London: British Film Institute, 1980).

Morse, Margaret, "Postsynchronising rock music and television," *Journal of Communication Inquiry*, vol. 10, no. 1 (Winter 1986), pp. 15–28.

Mulvey, Laura, "Visual pleasure and narrative cinema," *Screen*, vol. 16, no. 3 (Autumn 1975), pp. 6–18.

"Music directors' symposium," *Variety*, 14 March 1984, pp. 69–82.

Nowell-Smith, Geoffrey, "A note on history/discourse," *Edinburgh Magazine*, no. 1 (1976), pp. 26–32.

Orman, John, *The Politics of Rock Music* (Chicago: Nelson-Hall, 1984).

Peterson-Lewis, Sonja, and Chennault, Shirley A., "Black artists' music videos: three success strategies," *Journal of Communication*, vol. 36, no. 1 (Winter 1986), pp. 107–14.

Phelan, Margaret, "Panopticism and the uncanny: notes toward television's visual form," unpublished paper read at The Modern Language Association Convention, December 1986.

Phelan, Margaret, cf. Kaplan, E. Ann, and Phelan, Margaret, 1987.

Sobczak, Gene, "MTV, radio and unit sales," unpublished paper, Rutgers University, 1984.

Staiger, Janet, "Mass produced photoplays: economic and signifying practices in the first years of Hollywood," *Wide Angle*, vol. 4, no. 3 (1980), pp. 12–28.

Staiger, Janet, cf. Bordwell, David, Thompson, Kristen, and Staiger, Janet, 1985.

Stallybrass, Peter, and White, Allon, *The Politics and Poetics of Transgression* (London and New York: Methuen/Cornell, 1986).

Stam, Robert, "Television news," in E. Ann Kaplan, ed., *Regarding Television: Critical Approaches – An Anthology* (Los Angeles: American Film Institute, 1983), pp. 23–43.

Stern, Daniel N. "Mother and infant at play: the dyadic interaction involving facial, vocal and gaze behaviors," in Michael Lewis and L.A. Rosenblaum, eds, *The Origins of Behavior: vol. I The Effect of the Infant on the Caregiver* (New York: Wiley, 1974).

Swenson, John, ed., *The Year in Rock, 1981–82* (New York: Putnam, 1981).

Tetzlaff, Dave, "MTV and the politics of postmodern pop," *Journal of Communication Inquiry*, vol. 10, no. 1 (Winter 1986), pp. 80–91.

Thompson, David, cf. Bordwell, David, Thompson, Kristin, and Staiger, Janet, 1985.

Tribe, Keith, "History and the production of memories," *Screen*, vol. 18, no. 4 (Winter 1977/8), pp. 9–22.

White, Allon, cf. Stallybrass, Peter, and White, Allon, 1986.

Wright, Nick, "Pat Benatar," in John Swenson, ed., *The Year in Rock, 1981–82* (New York: Putnam, 1981).

Select glossary*

CINEMATIC VERSUS THE EXTRA-CINEMATIC   Keeping this distinction clearly in mind prevents us from falling into the trap of sociological critics, and linking screen image and lived experience too simplistically. The CINEMATIC refers to all that goes on on the screen and to what happens between screen image and spectator (what results from the cinematic apparatus). The EXTRA-CINEMATIC refers to discussion about, for example: the lives of the director, stars, producers, etc.; the production of the film in Hollywood, as an institution; the politics of the period when a film was made; and the cultural assumptions at the time a film was made.

CLASSICAL CINEMA   A controversial but convenient term referring to the feature-length narrative film made and distributed by the Hollywood studio system, roughly from 1925 through 1960. Central to the classical paradigm are conventions of film practice that are repeated from product to product (intentionally or not) and that the audience comes to rely upon and to expect. The characteristics of classical cinema can be determined on several levels: (1) in terms of *production*, the classical film can be categorized according to GENRE, stars, directors, producers (studios); (2) in terms of *narrative*, the classical film will have a tightly organized PLOT with clearly defined conflicts, ENIGMAS, cause—effect relationship, and a focus on individual characters; (3) in terms of *editing*, the classical film will adhere to the CONTINUITY system; and (4) in terms of *formal mechanisms*, the classical film will proceed by alternation and repetition (of its shots, camera set-ups, angles, signifying structures, such as editing patterns, reverse-angle, etc.)

*Courtesy of Rutgers Film Faculty, Sandy Flitterman-Lewis, and Miriam Hansen, who, along with E. Ann Kaplan, compiled the glossary from which these items are taken.

with a tendency toward balance, symmetry, and resolution such that the film appears to move inevitably from beginning to the point of closure. The latter two in particular are designed to produce a "reality effect," to create the illusion of reality for the spectator (cf. REALISM).

CLOSURE   A characteristic trait of classical narrative structure: we expect every element to be motivated, every event to have a cause (which will be explained in the course of the narrative), every conflict, ENIGMA and contradiction that the narrative sets up in the beginning to be resolved by the end.

CODE   A term used in SEMIOTICS (SEMIOLOGY) to describe a set of rules or conventions that structure a particular DISCOURSE. The cinema employs a complex system of codes pertaining to its heterogeneous levels of expression: codes of representation and editing, acting and narrative, codes of sound, be it music, speech or noise. Some of these codes are specific to the cinema (e.g. editing), some are shared with other forms of art and communication (e.g. codes of lighting and gesture with the theater, codes of narrative with the novel or short story).

CONNOTATION   The suggestive, associative, figurative sense of an expression (word, image, sign) that extends beyond its strict literal definition (DENOTATION), beyond what appears to be its "natural" meaning. In practice, denotative and connotative meanings cannot be that easily distinguished, especially when we are dealing with images.

CONTINUITY   A system of editing devised to bridge the gaps resulting from different camera setups, to stitch the spaces together in such a way that the spectator ignores the cuts ("invisible" editing); the continuity system subordinates space and time to the logic of narrative, action. Major conventions of continuity editing include: the 180 DEGREE RULE; the SHOT/REVERSE SHOT and POINT OF VIEW constructions, the latter depending on EYELINE MATCH; MATCH ON ACTION (or cutting movement); the 30 DEGREE RULE; an overall pattern of ESTABLISHING SHOT/breakdown/re-establishing shot.

DIEGESIS   (Greek for "recital of facts".) The denotative material of film narrative including the fictional space and time dimensions implied by the narrative; the fictive space and time into which the film works to absorb the spectator, the self-contained fictional world of the film.

DISCOURSE   Any social relation involving language or other sign systems as a form of exchange between participants, real or imaginary, particular or collective. Discursive exchange involves, as its points of reference, the conditions of expression, a source of articulation ("I") as well as an addressee ("you"), not necessarily explicit but always implied by the discursive structure. A discourse is shared by a socially constituted group of speakers; it defines the terms of what can or can't be said and extends beyond verbal language to a range of fields in which meaning is culturally organized (e.g. art, ideology).

FREUD AND THE OEDIPAL CRISIS   Before going on to discuss the mechanisms underlying pleasure in the cinema, it is necessary to outline

Freud's notion of the Oedipus complex, which provided the cornerstone for his (at the time) revolutionary psychoanalytic theory and on which the other phenomena relevant to film theory depend.

Freud took the name Oedipus from classical mythology, particularly the story, dramatized by Sophocles, of how Oedipus unwittingly killed his father and married his mother, a deed for which he was severely punished. The myth represents for Freud the inevitable fantasy of the growing child: first bound in illusory unity with his mother, whom he does not recognize as Other, separate, or different, the child exists blissfully in a pre-Oedipal phase; as he moves into the phallic phase, the child becomes aware of his father. At the height of his positive Oedipal phase, he loves his mother and hates his father who takes mother for himself. Successful resolution of this Oedipal phase takes place on the boy's discovery that his mother lacks the penis, i.e. is castrated (he can only imagine that all people must originally have had penises). This bitter discovery propels him away from his mother, since he fears that by identifying with the one who lacks the penis, he will endanger his own organ. He now identifies with his father, whom he longs to be like, and he looks forward to "finding someone like his mother" to marry.

Freud did not pay much attention to the girl's Oedipal crisis, but post-Freudians have generally agreed that it is a much more complicated one. They argue that the girl turns away from her mother through penis envy and the belief that her mother is responsible for her lack of a penis. The girl tries to get from the father what the mother could not provide, now equating "child" with "penis," and looking to bear the child with a man like her father.

IDEOLOGY   While for Marx IDEOLOGY referred to the ideological components of all bourgeois institutions and modes of production, recent film critics have rather followed Althusser for whom IDEOLOGY is a series of representations and images, reflecting the conceptions of "reality" that any society assumes. IDEOLOGY thus no longer refers to beliefs people consciously hold but to the myths that a society lives by, as if these myths referred to some natural, unproblematic "reality."

LACAN'S IMAGINARY AND SYMBOLIC   Some aspects of Lacan have been useful in film theory because he combined Freudian psychoanalysis with semiology, thus offering a means for linking semiotic and psycho-analytic readings of films. Lacan's insight was to rephrase Freudian theory by using a linguistic model for the movement between different stages, as against the non-linguistic, essentially biological and developmental Freudian model. Lacan's concept of the imaginary corresponds (roughly) to Freud's pre-Oedipal phase, although the child is already a signifier, already inserted in a linguistic system. But the world of the imaginary is nevertheless *for the child* a prelinguistic moment, a moment of illusory unity with the mother, whom he does not know as Other. The Lacanian child is forced to move on from the world of the imaginary, not because of the literal threat of castration but because he acquires language, which is based on the concept of "lack." He enters the world of the symbolic governed by the Law of the Father and revolving around the phallus as signifier. Here, in language, he discovers that he is an object in a realm of signifiers that circulate around the Father (= phallus). He learns discourse and the different "I" and "You" positions. The illusory unity with the Mother is broken partly by the mirror phase, with the child's recognition of the Mother as a separate image/entity, and of himself as an image (ego-ideal), creating the structure of the divided subject; and partly by introduction of the Father as a linguistic Third Term, breaking the mother—child dyad. Although the child now lives in the symbolic, he still longs for the world of the imaginary; it is this longing that the experience of the cinema partly satisfies, particularly in the sense of providing the more perfect selves (ego-ideals) evoked by the mirror phase and facilitating a regression to that phase.

METAPHOR   A figure of speech (a TROPE) consisting of two parts (traditionally called tenor and vehicle) expressing and creating a relation of comparison between two ordinarily unrelated elements, e.g. "the windmills of the mind."

MONTAGE   (French for "assembling" or "putting together".) Editing, usually referring to traditions outside the CONTINUITY system (e.g. Soviet cinema of the 1920s). In Hollywood films, montage sequences (sequences "telescoping" historical events, newspaper headlines, etc.) usually stand out by contrast to the dominant continuity style of editing.

180 DEGREE SYSTEM or RULE   Crucial to the CONTINUITY style in editing, this convention dictates that the camera remain on one side of an invisible line, the line of action or 180 degree line, thereby ensuring screen direction and general spatial orientation for the spectator. Movement of characters, objects or the camera automatically involves a re-establishing of the 180 degree space.

PLOT   The discursive organization of a NARRATIVE, i.e. the filmic actualization of narrative events. In contrast to the mental reconstruction of events which comprises a film's STORY, plot refers to the order and manner in which events are presented in the film itself. Story and plot *can* coincide, but they usually differ; the plot may alter the sequence (e.g. flashback), duration (e.g. a life time), and frequency (e.g. a repeated action) of events as they have presumably occurred in the story.

REALISM   (1) A summary term comprising literary and artistic conventions that have their origin in the first half of the nineteenth century; (2) in the cinema, an unspoken agreement between filmmaker and audience to accept certain modes of representation and narrative as "realistic," "faithful to reality," which implies a temporary belief in the "transparence" of the film, the three-dimensionality of the space projected on the screen, and in the "presence" of events unfolding, as if for the first time, before our eyes; (3) a style of filmmaking which attempts to approximate the look of reality (Bazin: "to recreate the world in its own image"), with emphasis on authentic locations and details, long shots and lengthy takes, eye-level placement of camera, a minimum of editing and special effects; often involving an effort to efface the traces of the film's construction, of the intervention on the part of the filmmaker.

REPRESENTATION   This concept indicates the "constructed" nature of the image, which Hollywood mechanisms strive to conceal. The dominant Hollywood style, realism (an apparent imitation of the social world we live in), hides the fact that a film is constructed, and perpetuates the illusion that spectators are being shown what is "natural." The half-aware "forgetting" that the spectator engages in allows the pleasurable mechanisms of voyeurism and fetishism to flow freely.

SEMIOLOGY, SEMIOTICS   (from the Greek root *sem*-, sign). A discipline devoted to the study of SIGNs, the basic unit of meaning in a process of SIGNIFICATION. Semiology or semiotics (depending on whether the particular approach is derived from the model of Structural Linguistics (Saussure) or from American Pragmatism (Peirce)) studies the systems of signs that enable human beings to communicate, to enter into discursive relations. All cultural utterances (in a broad sense, not just verbal utterances) are enabled as well as limited by systems or CODEs that are shared by all who make and understand them; semiology/semiotics attempts to describe the underlying patterns which structure those utterances.

SIGN, SIGNIFICATION   In SEMIOLOGY/SEMIOTICS, the sign is the basic unit in the process of signification, the process of articulating and conveying meaning. The sign has two aspects, the "signifier" (the material shape – sound, image – which carries meaning) and the "signified" (the concept signified, which in turn may refer to a potentially infinite number of "referents").

VOYEURISM   A psychoanalytic term referring to the erotic gratification of watching someone without being seen oneself; the activity of the Peeping Tom. As a clinical perversion, voyeurism is the active counterpart to EXHIBITIONISM, practiced primarily by men with the female body as the object of the gaze. Given the spatial and representational organization of CLASSICAL cinema, voyeurism is a crucial component of the pleasure offered to the spectator.

Index

191

INDEX

195